THE MAGIC
WORKBOOK

THE MAGIC WORKBOOK

THE TOOLS YOU NEED TO TRANSFORM YOUR COMPANY

Donald J. Klein

Jim Zawacki

Michigan State University Press

East Lansing

∞The paper used in this publication meets the minimum requirements of
ANSI/NISO Z39.48–1992 (R 1997) (Permanence of Paper).

Michigan State University Press
East Lansing, Michigan 48823-5202

04 03 02 01 00 99 1 2 3 4 5 6

Book Design by Michael J. Brooks.
Cover Design by Heidi Dailey.

Visit Michigan State University Press on the World-Wide Web at:
        www.msu.edu/unit/msupress

CONTENTS

ACKNOWLEDGMENTS

We would like to thank all those associates at GR Spring and Stamping Inc., who helped develop the systems and many of the forms in this workbook. Special thanks to Verna and Christine, who helped prepare the final forms.

The Magic Workbook, Michigan State University Press, 1999

INTRODUCTION

We are asked by almost every visitor to our plant, "Where did you start? How did you go about changing Magic into a caring, fair, profitable, and vital place to work?" This workbook will answer those questions. If you have read the companion volume to this Workbook, *It's Not Magic,* you will be familiar with our story. If not, suffice it to say that Magic is a real company—GR Spring & Stamping, Inc., a supplier to the auto industry and other key manufacturers. Its transformation was brought about by real people using the tools described in this workbook, which will give you a general overview of the things we did to transform a dying business into a global competitor.

Since implementing the ideas in this workbook, our on-time shipments are close to 100 percent. We have become a technology leader in our industry. We have had only one lost time accident in eleven years. We have reduced inventory by 30 percent and tripled our sales. We have no timeclocks and have implemented a lifelong education program for all associates that has won several national awards. Most important of all, we now have a culture committed to trust and continuous improvement. We average twelve implemented suggestions for improvement per employee every year. The continual progress amazes us, but it happened and continues to happen.

We are not smooth consultants once removed from reality. The material in this book works. Of course not all the ideas in this book will be applicable to your organization, but if you use only one of these tools, it will be worth the time it takes to read through this workbook. We realized how much time it would have saved us to have had—*in the beginning*—in one place all the forms and processes, charts and checklists we eventually used at Magic. We have given you the no-nonsense, blunt guidelines we have tried and found successful. Now you understand why we felt that to tell the story of Magic (what we did in *It's Not Magic*) was not enough. We had to make it as easy as possible for others to change as Magic did. It *is* possible.

Where did we begin at Magic? By establishing a *culture* that would allow an accelerated rate of change to be successfully implemented. You can read books on world-class manufacturing concepts such as lean production, re-engineering, just-in-time, total quality management, empowerment, theory of constraints, chaos management, and so forth. They do not address the real issue of fundamentally changing a culture.

Changing a culture is a difficult and long-term process, like the tough bamboo nut that needs five years of nurturing and fertilizing before the shoot breaks through the ground and grows ninety feet in just six weeks. Did the plant grow in six weeks or five years? An organization's culture needs the same nurturing and fertilizing before change and trust are an accepted norm for everyone's daily actions. Change and trust precede continuous improvement and all the rest.

You will have to choose the ideas applicable to your company and the sequence for implementing them. After building trust, we feel that workplace organization and safety come next. We believe that if management cannot manage workplace organization and safety then it cannot manage much else. Safety and workplace organization are direct expressions of management's concern for its workers. After that, it is up to you.

One of the key components of any organization's foundation has to be T.R.I.C. In the story of Magic, **T** stood for trust; **R** for relationship; **I** for integrity; and **C** for communication. We have set this acronym in a section by itself because we believe that it is, if not the key ingredient to developing a positive culture, then at least one of the major building blocks of any organization.

T = Trust
R = Relationship
I = Integrity
C = Communication

This is not some fancy slogan. It has to be believed and lived by the organization. Significant cultural change cannot occur unless top management is involved and leads the way. The leader has to lead the charge and provide the tools; setting goals is not enough.

One more thing. We urge you to contact us at zawacki@grs-s.com or kleind@gvsu.edu with your ideas and experiences. We certainly do not know everything—in fact, we continue to learn ways to improve this workbook. It will succeed only if it helps you, and we would like to know how we can improve it. The magic of a smoothly running organization is not limited to Magic, Inc. We want you to experience it for yourself.

Don Klein
Jim Zawacki

TRUST

Trust is a foundation difficult to build, but it is absolutely necessary for any relationship to grow. Since growing people should be any organization's number one goal, it is imperative that management understand and practice trust. Assessing whether or not an organization has trust is relatively easy. If there is trust, then honest relationships, integrity, and communication are givens. Over and over we hear that management does not communicate. What have you done to build trust, understanding, and communication?

You build trust by doing what you say you are going to do. If you promise to start meetings on time, then do not reward latecomers by waiting for them. If you promise to implement or complete something by a specific time, then do it on time. A promise unkept is an obligation unpaid. Do not lie. Make few promises; keep the ones you make. Listen and speak with empathy. Deal with people consistently. You have to build trust moment by moment.

The chief executive must be able to trust all subordinate leaders. Trust is difficult for leaders who feel that they have to micromanage. Nontrusting leaders do not nurture subleaders or give them the opportunity to exercise their full creative talents. Trust has to be balanced with a willingness to remove people who cannot be trusted. Without trust and mutual respect among leaders and associates, an organization will combine low performance and low morale.

T.R.I.C. (presented in the Introduction) guided us and our conduct. We used those four simple words to create a family atmosphere where all our associates have the chance to grow. Even then, not everyone has bought into T.R.I.C.

TRUST:

- Assured reliance on the character, ability, or truth of someone or something
- One in which confidence is placed
- Dependence on something in the future or contingent

RULES OF TRUST:

- Trust is not blind
- Trust needs boundaries
- Trust demands learning
- Trust is tough
- Trust needs bonding
- Trust needs touch
- Trust requires leadership

RELATIONSHIP:

- The state of being related or interrelated
- The connections or bindings among participants in a relationship—kinship

INTEGRITY:

- Doing what you say you will do
- Firm adherence to a code of especially moral or artistic values: incorruptibility
- An unimpaired condition: soundness
- The quality or state of being complete or undivided: completeness

COMMUNICATION:

- An act or instance of transmitting *and* receiving
- Information transferred by verbal or written message
- A process whereby information is exchanged through a system of commonly understood symbols
- A system for communicating—phones, computers—a technique for expressing ideas

T. R. I. C.

<u>T</u>RUST

<u>R</u>ELATIONSHIP

<u>I</u>NTEGRITY

<u>C</u>OMMUNICATION

Significant cultural change cannot take place until top management is convinced that change is necessary and is dedicated to make it happen.

The Magic Workbook, Michigan State University Press, 1999

HOUSEKEEPING/WORKPLACE ORGANIZATION

If you cannot manage housekeeping or safety, you cannot manage anything else. Housekeeping and safety are direct expressions of management's concern for its employees. They also indicate respect for one's associates. Sometimes called workplace organization, housekeeping is associated with cleanliness and the belief that everything has a home and should be there or in use. Organization means eliminating wasted time and materials and superfluous activities. Housekeeping is a good place to start because it involves everyone and has a positive effect on Key Performance Indicators—quality, cost, delivery, safety, and morale. You will not find many programs that can have as many positive effects on as many areas as good housekeeping.

Some ideas and actions we have tried:

- A cross-functional committee is formed that includes a high-level manager to lessen red tape and minimize levels of approval, so that it can make go or no-go decisions on the spot. The committee's purpose is to oversee, continuously improve, and promote the expectations of workplace organization.
- Top management gives the committee an initial mission statement as a starting point. The committee then develops its own vision, mission, value statement, and annual plans. These statements and plans are reviewed by top management for consistency with corporate goals.
- Trained workplace organization auditors conduct weekly audits of the entire facility.
- The Workplace Organization Committee works diligently to achieve consistency among auditors. Some auditors tend to give higher scores, while others give lower scores for the same thing. Training and constant committee monitoring help bring consistency and fairness to the process.
- Weekly audited performance scores and comments are posted in respective work areas.
- A facilities-wide scoreboard compares all areas' results.
- Common usage areas are assigned to specific work areas and are scored as a part of that work area.
- Each work area and department has its own individualized performance measurements.
- At the end of each month, the work area or department with the highest score is treated to a lunch at the company or tickets to a movie or sporting event during the next month.

WARNING: It is easier for some departments to score higher than others. Be sure to select measurements that make it challenging for all areas. You might have to choose a winner based on the percentage of improvement since the last measurement. It is usually easier for the office to keep things picked up and clean than the tool-room.

- We have a spring cleanup contest. The individuals who collect the most trash outdoors are recognized with small prizes such as shirts, caps, jackets, and so forth. A cookout served by management usually follows the cleanup.
- We play find the "Treasure Trash." Over the plantwide communication system we announce that the workplace committee has hidden an item that is out of place. The first person who discovers the item receives $20 at one of our next plantwide celebrations.

An organization should not have to announce a cleanup the day before visitors arrive. Personal satisfaction and pride are the main reasons for housekeeping, and a workplace should be presentable all the time. Everyone feels better when a place is well lighted, bright, clean, and organized. Visitors are impressed when they walk into a place that has the basics organized. Workplace organization, besides being just good business, provides a sense of pride and increased self-worth for everyone.

Magic, Inc.

SOME REASONS FOR BEING "FETISH" ABOUT HOUSEKEEPING

1. It is the "right thing" to do because it increases the quality of life for everyone.

2. It increases safety for everyone.

3. It promotes the health of employees.

4. It provides increased worker satisfaction and productivity, as everything has a home.

5. It improves everyone's self-esteem.

6. It is a pride builder for the workers and the company.

7. It is a strong marketing tool.

8. It is a good public relations tool regarding visitors to our company.

9. It increases quality and lessens worker frustrations.

10. It reduces the investment in equipment and tools and in general lowers operating expenses.

11. It frees up space for other uses and defers investment for such space.

12. What else can you add to the list?

WORKPLACE ORGANIZATION INSPECTION FORM

ITEMS TO BE INSPECTED	# Good	div/#viewed	SCORE
1 Are desktops organized and free of excess clutter and are shelves arranged neatly?	9	11	82
Are there boxes on desks? Do the shelves look cluttered? *A few need a little organizing*			
2 Are the areas under the desks free of boxes, etc?			100
Looks Good Are boxes being stored under desks? Recycle boxes are okay if they are not overflowing.			
3 Is the comparator clear of parts not currently being measured?			90
Is the comparator off with no one around, and are parts setting on it? *Work in process*			
4 Are boxes in sample storage area by Toolroom office labeled and stacked neatly?			98
2 labels NOT showing from front Does it look as if there is some form of organization, or are things just put anywhere on shelves?			
5 Is inside and top of coat closet neatly organized?			100
Is the closet clean and organized? Is there clutter stored there?			
6 Is the recycle box overflowing?	4	5	90
Does the box need to be emptied?			
7 Is main bulletin board and Fax/Printer area neat/organized?			100
Is the board organized or cluttered? What about the cart the fax machine sits on?			
8 Are corporate KPI charts/boards organized and up-to-date?			98
Are charts arranged in an orderly fashion? Are they current? *One was out to date*			
9 Are the EDM benches neat and organized?	2	3	90
Are the workbenches cluttered? Do they look organized? *Work in process*			
10 Are the racks in the EDM room neat and free of clutter?			98
Is there organization to them, or are things just put anywhere?			
		TOTAL	

Inspected By: *Michael Sanders*

Date: *1/15/98*

90-100	Excellent
80-90	Good
70-80	Fair
60-70	Needs Improvement
50-60	Poor

The Magic Workbook, Michigan State University Press, 1999

WORKPLACE ORGANIZATION INSPECTION FORM

ITEMS TO BE INSPECTED	# Good	div/#viewed	SCORE
1 Are desktops organized and free of excess clutter and are shelves arranged neatly?			
Are there boxes on desks? Do the shelves look cluttered?			
2 Are the areas under the desks free of boxes, etc?			
Are boxes being stored under desks? Recycle boxes are okay if they are not overflowing.			
3 Is the comparator clear of parts not currently being measured?			
Is the comparator off with no one around, and are parts setting on it?			
4 Are boxes in sample storage area by Toolroom office labeled and stacked neatly?			
Does it look as if there is some form of organization, or are things just put anywhere on shelves?			
5 Is inside and top of coat closet neatly organized?			
Is the closet clean and organized? Is there clutter stored there?			
6 Is the recycle box overflowing?			
Does the box need to be emptied?			
7 Is main bulletin board and Fax/Printer area neat/organized?			
Is the board organized or cluttered? What about the cart the fax machine sits on?			
8 Are corporate KPI charts/boards organized and up-to-date?			
Are charts arranged in an orderly fashion? Are they current?			
9 Are the EDM benches neat and organized?			
Are the workbenches cluttered? Do they look organized?			
10 Are the racks in the EDM room neat and free of clutter?			
Is there organization to them, or are things just put anywhere?			
		TOTAL	

Inspected By: _____	90-100	Excellent
	80-90	Good
	70-80	Fair
Date: _____	60-70	Needs Improvement
	50-60	Poor

WORKPLACE ORGANIZATION INSPECTION FORM

ITEMS TO BE INSPECTED	#Good	div/#viewed	SCORE
1 Are the paper and metal barrels running over with material?			
Are barrels overflowing? Is there trash on floor around barrels?			
2 Are the floors free of oil, debris, dirt, parts, etc.?			
Do floors need to be swept/mopped? Are there oil puddles on floor?			
3 Are all items (tools and utensils) in their proper locations?			
Are tools put away? Are tools cluttering area?			
4 Are lofts above front office and front conference room clean?			
Is there any organization to these rooms?			
5 Are the workbenches neat and cleaned?			
Are tools put away? Is there paperwork just thrown on desks? Pop cans/bottles?			
6 Are all of the cribs and cabinets clean and organized?			
Is there organization to these, or are things just put in any open space?			
7 Is the "West" air compressor room clean and organized?			
Are barrels arranged neatly? Are they labeled? Are shelves kept neat and clean?			
8 Is the "East" air compressor room clean and organized?			
Are shelves kept neat and clean? Is room neat and uncluttered?			
9 Is the bulletin board and electrical cart clean and organized?			
Is there organization to the bulletin board? Is electrical cart free of clutter?			
10 Is loft above Systems office clean and organized?			
Are shelves arranged neatly? Is there organization to them? Are cleaning supplies stored neatly?			
		TOTAL	

Inspected By: _____

Date: _____

90-100	Excellent
80-90	Good
70-80	Fair
60-70	Needs Improvement
50-60	Poor

WORKPLACE ORGANIZATION INSPECTION FORM

ITEMS TO BE INSPECTED	#Good	div/#viewed	SCORE
1 Is the Q.A. Manager's office neat and organized?			n/a
Are desk and table neat and uncluttered?			
2 Is the Quality Assurance office neat and organized?			
Are desks neat and uncluttered? Is printer area neat and organized?			
3 Is the desk in file room neat and organized?			
Is there excess clutter? Know difference between working mess and clutter.			
4 Are the trash barrels filled with excess material?			
Comments			
5 Is Q.A. file room neat and organized?			
Does floor need vacuuming? Is the copy area neat/clean? Is stuff being stored on cabinets?			
6 Is the reject hold area clean and organized?			
Are boxes placed here in an orderly manner?			
7 Is surface plate in Q.A. shipping free of clutter?			n/a
Is there equipment setting on it?			
8 Are cabinets in Q.A. shipping clean and organized?			
Are cabinets neat, or are things just put in any open space? Could you find anything?			
9 Is sample board in Q.A. shipping neat and organized?			
Are parts set up in neat manner? Is there organization?			
10 Are corporate KPI charts & boards organized and up to date?			
Are charts in organized fashion? Are they current?			

		TOTAL

Inspected By: _____	90-100	Excellent
	80-90	Good
	70-80	Fair
Date: _____	60-70	Needs Improvement
	50-60	Poor

WORKPLACE ORGANIZATION INSPECTION FORM

ITEMS TO BE INSPECTED	# Good	div/#viewed	SCORE
1 Are the trash barrels running over with material?			
Are barrels overflowing? Is there trash/scrap around the floor?			
2 Are the floors free of oil, debris, dirt, parts, etc.?			
Are there oil puddles? Does floor need to be swept/mopped?			
3 Are the HiLo's clean and free of excess items?			
Do HiLos need cleaning? Are there dirty gloves, trash, etc being stored on HiLos?			
4 Are the workstations and scales clean and organized?			
Are work areas organized? Is there trash or pop bottles lying around?			
5 Is the staple area clean and organized?			
Is area arranged neatly? Are there bands on the floor?			
6 Is the raw storage area clean and organized?			
Is area kept neat and organized?			
7 Is ground outside of front docks clean and free of clutter?			
Is area clean and free of trash/cigarette butts?			
8 Is the customer service office clean and organized?			
Are desks neat and organized? What about printer areas?			
9 Is the back dock area clean and organized?			
Is back dock area free of clutter? Are skids just placed anywhere, or in an organized fashion?			
10 Is finished goods aisleway (boxes/skids) organized?			
Is area neat and organized? Are aisleways free of boxes/skids?			

TOTAL

Inspected By: _____

Date: _____

90-100	Excellent
80-90	Good
70-80	Fair
60-70	Need Improve
50-60	Poor

WORKPLACE ORGANIZATION INSPECTION FORM

ITEMS TO BE INSPECTED	#Good	div/#viewed	SCORE
1 Are paper and metal barrels running over with material?			
Are barrels overflowing? Is there trash/scrap around barrel on floor?			
2 Are the floors free of oil, debris, dirt, parts, etc.?			
Are there oil puddles? Does floor need to be swept or mopped?			
3 Are all items (tools, pans, pallet jack, & utensils) in proper locations?			
Are items just put anywhere/in aisleways?			
4 Are machines free of excess items and scrap, and are they clean?			
Are machines clean? Are there dirty rags lying around?			
5 Are the workbenches and toolboxes neat and cleaned?			
SPC benches neat and organized?			
6 Are all of the liquid containers properly labeled?			
Are all liquid containers legibly labeled?			
7 Are SPC gage cabinets organized and instruments cleaned?			
Is there organization to cabinets, or are things just put where they will fit?			
8 Is the hot corner clean and organized?			
Is there organization to bulletin board? Are charts up to date?			
9 Is floor around oven and oven top and sink area (filter) clean?			
Are areas clean? Are there parts lying around?			
10 Is the sanding belt area clean and organized?			
Are machines clean and free of scrap? What about the floor?			

TOTAL

	90-100	Excellent
Inspected By: _____	80-90	Good
	70-80	Fair
Date: _____	60-70	Needs Improvement
	50-60	Poor

<u>WORKPLACE ORGANIZATION INSPECTION FORM</u>

ITEMS TO BE INSPECTED	#Good	div/#viewed	SCORE
1 Are the paper and metal barrels running over with material?			
Are barrels overflowing? Is scrap/trash around barrel on floor?			
2 Are the floors free of oil, debris, dirt, parts, etc.?			
Are there oil puddles/scrap/parts/etc. on floors? Do they need to be swept/mopped?			
3 Are all items (tools, utensils, and chairs) in their proper locations?			
Are there tools on machines/oven/spc bench?			
4 Are machines free of excess items and scrap, and are guards clean?			
Do machines need to be cleaned? Is there scrap on them?			
5 Is excess equipment stocked in its proper place?			
Are there spare coils lying in aisleway?			
6 Are all of the liquid containers properly labeled?			
Do all containers have a legible label? Do you know what is in each just by looking at container?			
7 Are SPC gage cabinets and desk organized and instruments cleaned?			
Is there organization to cabinet? SPC desk neat? Calipers/Comparator clean?			
8 Is strap machine free of parts and clean?			
Is strap machine clean? Are there parts on it and all around it on the floor?			
9 Are the die racks clean and organized?			
Is rack area clean/organized, or are dies just put in any open space?			
10 Is the hot corner clean and organized?			
Are KPIs arranged neatly, and are they current?			**TOTAL**

	90-100	Excellent
Inspected By: _____	80-90	Good
	70-80	Fair
Date: _____	60-70	Needs Improvement
	50-60	Poor

Front offices also include General Manager, Accountant, Sales, President, and the front conference room.

WORKPLACE ORGANIZATION INSPECTION FORM			
ITEMS TO BE INSPECTED	# Good	div/#viewed	SCORE
1 Are the desktops organized and free from excess clutter?			
Know difference between working mess vs. clutter			
2 Are the areas under the desks free of boxes, etc?			
Recycle boxes okay. No other boxes.			
3 Are all of the wastebaskets running over with trash?			
Is trash overflowing?			
4 Are the recycle boxes overflowing?			
Comments			
5 Are floors free of debris, dirt, paperclips, staples, etc?			
Do floors need to be vacuumed?			
6 Is inside and top of the coat closet neatly organized?			
Is there any type of organization to closet? Does it need to be cleaned out?			
7 Are items on shelves, top of dividers, and bookshelves arranged neatly?			
Do dividers and bookshelves look cluttered?			
8 Are office machines free of excess items and paper, are they clean?			
Is there excess material around machines? Do machines need to be cleaned?			
9 Is the front lobby neat and clean?			
How does our lobby look to customers? Is it clean & organized?			
10 Is the posted material in a neat and orderly manner?			
Are KPIs posted neatly? What about other information?			
		TOTAL	

	90-100	Excellent
Inspected By: _____	80-90	Good
	70-80	Fair
Date: _____	60-70	Needs Improvement
	50-60	Poor

WORKPLACE ORGANIZATION INSPECTION FORM

ITEMS TO BE INSPECTED	#Good	div/#viewed	SCORE
1 Are paper and metal barrels running over with material?			
Are barrels overflowing? Is there trash/scrap on floor around barrel?			
2 Are floors free of oil, scrap, slugs, debris, and metal shavings?			
Are there oil puddles on the floor? Does floor need to be swept/mopped?			
3 Are the liquid containers properly labeled?			
Are liquid containers labeled legibly?			
4 Are machines free of excess items and scrap, and are they clean?			
Are there extra tools lying around? Are there metal shavings on or around machines?			
5 Are cabinets and workbenches clean and organized?			
Is there organization to these areas, or are they cluttered?			
6 Are brooms and mop buckets in their proper place?			
Are brooms/mop buckets just sitting anywhere or are they in designated area?			
7 Is the steel rack clean and organized?			
Is there some type of organization to the rack?			
8 Is the welding area clean and organized?			
Is area clean and uncluttered? Does floor need to be swept?			
9 Are the main aisleways clean and uncongested?			
Is there anything that is blocking aisleways?			
10 Is the toolroom office clean and organized?			
Are desks clean and uncluttered? Is bulletin board neat and organized?		**TOTAL**	

	90-100	Excellent
Inspected By: _____	80-90	Good
	70-80	Fair
Date: _____	60-70	Needs Improvement
	50-60	Poor

MONTHLY WORK PLACE ORGANIZATION SCORES - 1997/98

	Month	FS	ST	TR	MNT	SH	QA	ENG	FO	Magic
1st Qtr	July	**103.2**	98.4	97.6	98.6	98.6	98.0	98.3	98.9	98.95
	August	98.7	99.0	98.5	98.8	98.9	98.9	98.6	**99.5**	98.86
	September	95.4	98.3	99.2	98.1	99.0	**99.3**	98.0	99.2	98.31
2nd Qtr	October	98.0	96.2	96.8	95.2	**100.0**	95.7	94.2	98.8	96.86
	November	85.0	88.6	90.9	89.8	**94.4**	93.4	88.2	**94.4**	90.59
	December	88.4	89.3	90.3	90.2	96.5	96.6	**103.2**	95.2	93.71
3rd Qtr	January	82.6	83.8	86.8	90.1	88.2	**95.0**	92.7	90.4	88.70
	February	89.7	93.8	89.6	91.7	94.4	95.2	93.3	**96.9**	93.08
	March	91.5	**102.9**	93.4	97.6	94.8	97.8	94.7	93.8	95.81
4th Qtr	April	91.1	92.4	92.6	87.8	92.9	**95.7**	92.6	95.6	92.59
	May	96.0	98.4	**103.9**	96.6	94.2	97.5	95.3	97.3	97.40
	June	93.7	95.2	91.7	**97.3**	95.9	93.4	94.3	95.1	94.58
	YTD Avg	92.8	94.7	94.3	94.3	95.7	96.4	95.3	96.3	94.95

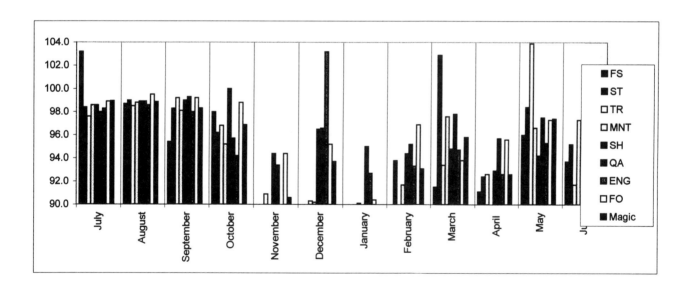

Workplace Organization Scores by Department

FOURSLIDE

WEEK	1	2	3	4	5	BP	MON. AVG
July	99.8	99.0	88.0	97.2	99.4	32.5	103.2
August	99.0	99.4	99.5	96.8	*	*	98.7
September	90.0	99.0					
October							
November							
December							
January							
February							
March							
April							
May							
June							
Weekly Avg	96.3	99.1	93.8	97.0	99.4	32.5	100.9

SPRING TORSION

WEEK	1	2	3	4	5	BP	MON. AVG
July	99.4	98.8	96.0	97.8	100.0		98.4
August	99.4	99.6	99.0	97.8	*	*	99.0
September	96.5	99.2					
October							
November							
December							
January							
February							
March							
April							
May							
June							
Weekly Avg	98.4	99.2	97.5	97.8	100.0	#####	98.7

TOOLROOM

WEEK	1.0	2.0	3.0	4.0	5.0	BP	MON. AVG
July	99.0	99.2	92.0	98.2	99.8	0.0	97.6
August	98.2	99.6	98.8	97.2	*	*	98.5
September	95.5	99.2					
October							
November							
December							
January							
February							
March							
April							
May							
June							
Weekly Avg	97.6	99.3	95.4	97.7	99.8	0.0	98.0

MAINTENANCE

WEEK	1.0	2.0	3.0	4.0	5.0	BP	MON. AVG
July	99.6	98.3	96.0	99.2	100.0	0.0	98.6
August	98.8	99.6	99.8	96.8	*	*	98.8
September	96.3	99.4					
October							
November							
December							
January							
February							
March							
April							
May							
June							
Weekly Avg	98.2	99.1	97.9	98.0	100.0	0.0	98.7

SHIPPING

WEEK	1	2	3	4	5	BP	MON. AVG
July	99.4	100.0	95.0	98.9	99.6	0.0	98.6
August	99.2	99.6	99.3	97.6	*	*	98.9
September	98.3	98.7					
October							
November							
December							
January							
February							
March							
April							
May							
June							
Weekly Avg	99.0	99.4	97.2	98.3	99.6	0.0	98.8

QUALITY

WEEK	1	2	3	4	5	BP	MON. AVG
July	99.8	99.2	93.7	99.3	99.8	0.0	98.0
August	99.0	99.8	99.3	97.4	*	*	98.9
September	98.5	99.3					
October							
November							
December							
January							
February							
March							
April							
May							
June							
Weekly Avg	99.1	99.4	96.5	98.4	99.8	0.0	98.4

ENGINEERING

WEEK	1	2	3	4	5	BP	MON. AVG
July	98.6	99.2	95.0	99.2	99.4	0.0	98.3
August	99.0	99.4	99.2	96.8	*	*	98.6
September	95.5	98.6					
October							
November							
December							
January							
February							
March							
April							
May							
June							
Weekly Avg	97.7	99.1	97.1	98.0	99.4	0.0	98.4

FRONT OFFICES

WEEK	1	2	3	4	5	BP	MON. AVG
July	99.6	99.4	96.0	99.6	99.8	0.0	98.9
August	99.4	99.6	99.8	99.2	*	*	99.5
September	99.0	99.4					
October							
November							
December							
January							
February							
March							
April							
May							
June							
Weekly Avg	99.3	99.5	97.9	99.4	99.8	0.0	99.2

MAGIC, INC.

FISCAL 1997/98 WPO SCORES

DISTRIBUTE TO:

Dan Sheldon	Eric Smead	Mike Langly
Brian Zinderman	Dennis Morgan	Rob Deringer
Peter Thompson	Christine Andrews	Tom Pernie
Tim Lee	Mary Halls	

May 6, 1998

WORKPLACE ORGANIZATION TRAINING
MAGIC, INC.

Agenda
- Go over audit sheets
- Go over maps
- Plant walk-through if necessary

To Know:
- Audit folder back to Mary Halls by Thursday, noon.
- Always comment whenever points are taken away.
- Scores are figured by using percentages.

  -Example
      2 of 3 trash barrels are not overflowing
      2 divided by 3 is 66%

- You cannot look at everything in a department. This is an overview.
- Please be as objective and honest as possible.
- Try to look at all work areas as a customer would see it. Don't make excuses for disorganization.
- Remember, Workplace Organization is not only keeping things clean, it is organization as well. We can cut down on waste and improve productivity if we are honest with our scoring. We must stop working around the waste and eliminate it.
- Saying "I don't have time to get organized" is like saying, "I'm drowning, but I don't have time to swim."

SAFETY

Safety is the companion of workplace organization. Anyone that cannot manage this cannot manage anything else. It is a direct expression of management's concern for its associates. Giving attention to safety is the most obvious way for a company to walk the talk about the importance of people. When it comes to safety, you cannot allow yourself to become penny wise and dollar foolish. Any perceived safety issue is a real concern and important to associates. You may think things are safe, but only by listening to your associates will you be able to tell what is actually the case. Then you must spend the money to make the workplace safe in fact.

Some ideas and actions we have tried:

- A cross-functional committee is formed including a high-level manager, preferably the president, to minimize red tape and the need for complicated approvals, so that it can make go or no-go decisions on the spot.
- Top management gives the committee a mission statement as a starting point. The committee then develops its own vision, mission, value statement, and annual plans. These statements and plans are reviewed by top management for consistency with corporate goals.
- The committee meets at least once a month and provides minutes to key managers. The minutes are also posted on the various information boards to let associates see what has been discussed, as well as to make them more safety conscious.
- Every accident is posted and fully investigated and documented within twenty-four hours. The safety committee tries to determine ways of eliminating each type of accident. The president is contacted immediately if a serious accident occurs.
- A huge (six feet tall and about three feet wide) life-size poster of a character we call "Big John" is placed in a prominent place. Every accident is noted on Big John's body exactly where the person involved in the accident was hurt. The date, time, nature of the difficulty, and the individual's name are posted on Big John. Injuries are color coded as to their severity. Red implies an external injury requiring medical attention; yellow implies an internal injury requiring medical attention; and a large red color code implies that the injury caused missed days of work. This provides management with a Pareto analysis of accidents and sensitizes the associates to what is occurring, the need to be careful, and the need for suggestions on how to eliminate this type of problem.
- Measurements of the annual number of safety changes, dollars spent for safety improvements, and accident-free days all indicate the effectiveness of the safety program.

- At Magic, we issue safety buttons with the company's logo and statements like "Safety Counts" on them. Everyone is expected to wear the button every day at work. This is not only a personal reminder to everyone to work safely, but also a reminder to others who forget to wear theirs. Once a week someone from the safety committee randomly draws several associates' names. To the first two persons randomly chosen who are wearing their safety buttons goes some type of a safety gift, such as a first-aid kit, smoke detector and so forth. Each week the number of associates without buttons—the number of names drawn before two winners appear— is posted.
- At monthly luncheon celebrations, additional random safety button drawings are made, and gifts go to the first few wearing them.

- "Safety Bingo" is another game that helps make individuals more aware of safety. Cross-functional teams are chosen and numbers are drawn each day. All associates have their own bingo cards. Several rules promoting teamwork, safety, and attendance must be followed for people to use the daily numbers. See the attached set of bingo rules for further information. Prizes are given to the winner.

WARNING: Be sure you are not violating your state laws if you play safety bingo. Some states require registration to play bingo.

MAGIC, INC. SAFETY STATEMENT

The personal health and safety of each employee of this company is of primary importance. The prevention of occupational-induced injuries will be given precedence over operating productivity whenever necessary. To the greatest degree possible, management will provide the mechanical and physical facilities necessary for personal health and safety in keeping with the highest standards.

We will maintain a health and safety program conforming with the best practice of organizations of this type. To be successful, such a program must embody the proper attitudes toward injury and illness prevention on the part of both supervisors and associates. Only through such a cooperative effort can a safety record in the best interest of all be established and preserved.

Our objective is a health and safety program that will reduce the number of disabling injuries and illnesses to a minimum not merely in keeping with, but surpassing, the best experience of other operations similar to ours.

Our goal is zero accidents and injuries.

Our health and safety program includes:

- Providing mechanical and physical safeguards to the maximum extent that is possible;

- Conducting a program of health and safety inspections to find and eliminate unsafe working conditions and practices; to control health hazards; and to comply fully with the health and safety standards for every job;

- Training all employees in good health and safety practices;

- Developing and enforcing health and safety rules; requiring that employees cooperate with these rules as a condition of employment;

- Investigating promptly and thoroughly every accident to find its cause and correcting the problem so that it won't happen again.

We recognize that the responsibilities for health and safety are shared:

- The employer is responsible, and accepts the responsibility, for leadership of the health and safety program; for its effectiveness and improvement; and for providing the safeguards required to ensure safe working conditions;

- Supervisors are responsible for developing the proper attitudes toward health and safety in themselves and in those they supervise; and for ensuring that all operations are performed with the utmost regard for the health and safety of all personnel involved, including themselves;

- Associates are responsible for wholehearted, genuine cooperation with all aspects of the health and safety program, including compliance with all rules and regulations and for continuously practicing safety while performing their duties.

SIGNED *Mike Dillon* DATE 1/1/98

```
┌─────────────────────────┐
│                         │    *DATE:* _____
│   *INJURY REPORT*       │    This report must be completed and turned in to the office
│                         │    on the date of the injury.
└─────────────────────────┘
```

ASSOCIATE name: _____

Date of injury: _____ Time: _____

Type of injury (cut-burn-pinch-sliver-etc.)_____

Part of body injured: _____

What was the employee doing when the accident occured and how did it happen:

_____

_____

_____

_____

_____

Name the object or substance which injured the employee: _____

Was first aid administered in plant and what kind: _____

Administered by: _____

Was further medical attention needed: _____

If so, where was the employee taken, and by whom: _____

Associate's signature: _____

Supervisor's signature: _____

Signature of person filing report: _____

_____

Investigated by: _____Assigned date: _____

Was all of the above information correct: _____

How could this injury have been prevented and recommendations: _____

_____

_____

_____

_____

_____   Use back side if more
Signature of investigator and date turned in   Space is needed

SAFETY IS WORLD CLASS

The Magic Workbook, Michigan State University Press, 1999

SAFETY COMMITTEE MINUTES
7/8/98

Members:

    *Mike Dillion   *Roger Highman   *Tom Baker
    Ben Jones

        *indicates attending

NOTES:

1. Mike D. & Ben J. will review the storage of flammable materials.
2. Waste liquids - Mike D. & Ben J. will review recycling and disposal methods
3. Fourslide cheater bars and interlocks - Mike D/Ben J/Rob D.
4. Ben J. - status of guarding for MCT's?

TO DO LIST:

1. Safety Button drawing for June, Tom Baker.
2. Safety Walkarounds - postponed, will discuss again after end of the month.
3. Spill kits - Tom B. and Roger H. to make kits - need 10 kits to be completed by next Safety Meeting.

NEXT MEETING: *Wednesday, August 5, 1998, at 2:30 in the classroom.

AGENDA FOR NEXT MEETING:
    *Review above items

CC:

Members	Mike Langly	Material
Peter Thompson	F/S & S/T	Quality
Rod Berman	Toolroom	

CHRISTMAS TREE

B	I	N	G	O
1	16	32	49	66
2	17	33	50	67
3	18	FREE	51	68
4	19	34	52	69
5	20	35	53	70

The Magic Workbook, Michigan State University Press, 1999

SAFETY BINGO

The new bingo game will start on Monday NOV 16, 1998

Two numbers will be drawn per day until we get four winners.

Please see which group you belong to and remember the rules about any accidents. (Rules are attached).

The card pattern for this game is attached.

REMEMBER: IF YOUR CARD IS LOST OR STOLEN IT WILL NOT BE REPLACED DURING THE GAME, SO KEEP TRACK OF IT.

You have until the end of the workday to turn your winning card into the Safety Manager. If you are going to be gone, please have someone watch it for you.

As always, the numbers will be posted on the monitor and on the bulletin board. Good Luck and Remember to Work SAFE !!!!!!!!

SAFETY COMMITTEE

MAGIC, INC.- SAFETY BINGO

This new awareness program is designed to bring us a new enthusiasm about being safety conscious. This program has been patterned after similar ones in other work places, and tailored to suit our plant. This is how it works:

1)	Everyone will be assigned to a group which will consist of a cross section of all employees.
2)	The game will be played just like regular Bingo. Everyone will be issued one numbered and registered game board. The safety committee will keep the log of numbers. These are at no cost.
3)	A new number(s) will be drawn each morning (M-T-W-Th-F) and posted on the Bulletin Board at Bond and on the Bulletin Board System at Waldorf.
4)	The number of winners per game board will be announced at the beginning of each new game. For instance, the first game might take six single line winners and then continue toward a full board winner.
5)	In the event of a tie for the last or only prize, a flip of a coin or names drawn from a hat will determine the winner(s).
6)	You may win only once per game as a single line winner, and then continue to play toward a full board.
7)	A win must be reported to the safety committee before the end of your shift.
8)	You can only play the board that is assigned to you. You cannot play another employee's board for him/her.
9)	If you have "approved time off" such as vacation day(s), personal day(s), or not-scheduled -to-work day(s), it is your responsibility to give your card (prior to your absence) to a safety committee member to be played for you. No one else may play your card! If you forget to give your card to a member, rule 10 will apply.
10)	In the event you call in sick, are absent for any other reason without prior permission, or are off for all or part of the day for disciplinary reasons, you will be able to use the numbers drawn on those days after you return to work. If one of them makes you a winner, you can claim a prize if there is one left. If not, you are out of luck.
11)	Rules are subject to change or amendment only between games.
12)	Prizes will vary, and will not be announced prior to the game.
13)	If you lose your card you are out of luck until the next cards are issued

NOTE - All prizes are donated by the company in the interest of promoting safety awareness.

Everything so far seems quite easy. How can anyone <u>not</u> win, right? Well, here are the rules that will hopefully make us more safety conscious, and make the game more interesting.

<u>SAFETY GLASSES</u> - If you are found by a supervisor or safety committee member, in the plant during work hours, other than designated areas or designated times without your safety glasses on, you will not be able to use the next day's bingo number. If you are found in violation of this rule a second time during the same game period, you must surrender your card to the committee and wait until the next game's cards are distributed. See the attached page for designated areas and times.

<u>SAFETY SHOES OR UNSAFE PRACTICES</u> will not be a factor at this time. (Note rule 10, disciplinary time off).

<u>FIRST-AID TREATMENT</u> - If you become injured and require first-aid treatment as defined by OSHA, either in the plant or at a clinic, you as an individual will not be able to use the two consecutive days bingo numbers following the day of injury. If you injure yourself a second time during the same game board, you must surrender your card to the committee and wait until the next game's cards are distributed.

<u>MEDICAL TREATMENT</u> - If you are injured and require medical treatment as defined by OSHA, you as an individual must surrender your card to the safety committee and the group that you are assigned to must forfeit the next three consecutive days bingo numbers following the date of the injury. If any two persons within your group require medical treatment during the same game (including anyone who has already surrendered his/her card) the whole group must surrender their cards and wait until the next game's cards are distributed.

<u>LOST TIME INJURY</u> - If there is any injury that results in a "Lost Time Injury" (where the employee is <u>unable</u> to work) the game is totally halted for a period of no less than 60 days from the date of the injury. All cards must be turned in at this time and new cards will be issued when the game is resumed. Prizes will carry over.

IMPORTANT NOTE - It is our hope that you will not sacrifice your personal safety while playing this game. We want all employees to seek any and all first-aid or medical treatment needed for an injury. An injury requires the filing of an injury report and anyone caught <u>not</u> doing so will be subject to forfeiture of all game eligibility for a period of up to 90 days depending on the severity. Any and all inquiries concerning an injury and its severity must be brought to the attention of the safety committee as a group for a decision.

MAGIC, INC.

SAFETY BUTTON WINNERS

FOR THE MONTH OF

FEBUARY, 1998

Rob Deringer
Verna Coburn
Barb Cannon
Scarlett Morgan
Tim Smead
Gail Kameron

BIG JOHN

The Magic Workbook, Michigan State University Press, 1999

CRITICISM AND DISCIPLINE

Management that does not provide criticism and discipline is a robber—a stealer of opportunities to improve. Such management lacks integrity. Too many times people are elevated to a managerial role for their skills, because they are well-liked, and for their judgment and leadership potential. Yet they are not provided much, if any, education or training in how to manage—especially in how to deliver criticism or discipline. Our experience has been that managers like least to discipline people or confront them with a problem. It is a tough challenge. But how will you ever solve a problem if you do not confront it?

We have used a series of eight two-hour sessions to introduce managers to what criticism actually is. We give them hints about how to send criticism; what kind of environment helps people grow through criticism; and how to identify "energy vampires," "bad apples," and "dream killers"; and show them how role-playing can lead to learning. Six to twelve people is an acceptable class size; we prefer eight to ten. The smaller the group, the more participation and opportunity to role-play.

The following are some of the exercises and ideas we have used in our eight-session program on sending criticism and confronting conflicts.

CRITICISM/DISCIPLINE

SESSION # 1

We establish the underlying culture ideas with short stories and class exercises and discussions. What are the four generic goals of any organization, in priority order? The answer, in priority order: growing people; making money; having fun; and having lots of "mental sex." The first session is aimed at teaching people how to grow others as well as themselves. This session sets the tone and guidelines for the balance of the program.

After approximately one hour the group is paired off and asked to come back in twenty minutes to introduce each other. Too many times people who have worked together for years don't realize the rich background of their colleagues. This also is a safe thing to talk about the first time – "yourself." They are asked to share what makes the other person happy and mad, and what that person's dreams are. This allows the participants to get to know each other's preferences, nonpreferences, and interests. See the attached worksheet. **(Session # 1 – Exercise)**

Homework assignment is with a partner, chosen at random by some lottery system, to identify what they like and dislike about the organization. This starts to ask participants to take some risk and starts to address some issues that the organization needs to discuss. See homework exercise sheet. **(Session # 1 – Homework)**

DISCIPLINE
Homework # 1

Likes and Dislikes

1. What do you like best about this organization? Share why you like the things that you do.

2. Share what you dislike about this organization. Please provide your reasons for your dislikes.

DISCIPLINE

1..What makes you **smile**?

2. What makes you **mad**?

3. What is your **dream**?

The Magic Workbook, Michigan State University Press, 1999

CRITICISM/DISCIPLINE

SESSION # 2

The session starts with a review of the major culture points from session # 1 and then adds about twenty minutes of new culture thoughts. This session then identifies ways to send criticism. Participants are asked to read the list titled "Sending Criticism." (See **Session # 2 – Handout**) After reading this and asking for any comments, the group is paired randomly and asked to add at least one more item to the seven categories identified on the handout. The group then shares and discusses their additions. This usually causes a good discussion about the way the organization normally deals with problems and how they might consider changing. These additions are listed for everyone to see and at the start of Session # 3 a revised "Sending Criticism" list with their highlighted suggestions is given to them as a reference.

This session's second hour reviews and discusses the homework from Session # 1.

Homework for Session # 3 is given to the participants and they are randomly paired to do the homework as a team. The homework is to have each team develop at least two role-playing cases that identify problems that the organization is having difficulty in bettering. **(See Session # 2 – Homework)**

HELPFUL HINTS FOR "SENDING" CRITICISM

1. **WHEN CRITICIZING, CONCENTRATE ON DEVELOPING THE INDIVIDUAL.**
    a. One effective technique is to create an action plan as a guide for the individual to improve.
    b. Avoid making any criticism destructive or too personal.
    c. Concentrate on turning the session into a win-win situation, so the teammate, manager, and company gain.
    d. Criticize actions, not people.
    e. Be prepared (anticipate questions).
    f. Ask them how they would change things to improve the situation.
    g. Provide specific examples and alternatives for the criticized behavior.
    h. Be direct and to the point.
    i. Try to make as many positive statements as possible.

2. **OFTEN THE CRITICISM'S TONE, NOT THE EXACT WORDS SELECTED, PROVOKES AN EMPLOYEE.**
    a. Concentrate on establishing a constructive and positive tone.
        Example: Begin with phrases such as "These skills could enhance your repertoire and make you more effective" and "Here's how you can improve."
    b. Don't demean employees or make them feel that they are incapable of improving.
    c. Put yourself in teammate's shoes when planning your criticism and think about how you would feel if someone delivered those comments to you.
    d. Rehearse what you are going to say before the meeting.
    e. Make sure the meeting ends on a positive note.
    f. Always stay calm and in control.
    g. Always be specific.
    h. Choose a neutral location.
    i. Praise in public, criticize in private.
    j. No need to raise your voice in anger.
    k. Constantly monitor tone of voice and body language.
    l. Allow some cool down time period if possible.
    m. Respect an individual's space and don't physically get in their face.
    n. Walk through the situation so the worker knows what needs to be changed and why.

The Magic Workbook, Michigan State University Press, 1999

3. **INVOLVING THE TEAMMATE IN THE PROCESS SERVES AS ANOTHER WAY TO TURN THE EXPERIENCE INTO A REWARDING ONE:**
   Example: "Let's look at alternatives. Let's come up with solutions together."
   a. Avoid supplying all the answers.
   b. Avoid making sweeping statements.
      Example: Instead of saying, "You're messing up", a comment that makes the other person feel angry and helpless, offer suggestions on how to improve.
   c. How can you help me with this problem?
   d. How do you see this as affecting the team?
   e. What do you feel should be done?
   f. How long should it be before we evaluate this again?
   g. Ask them for their view of the problem (maybe they don't even believe there is a problem).
   h. How can I help?
   i. Ask for opinions first.

4. **FOCUS ON THE FUTURE, NOT THE PAST.**
   a. Stress partnership in trying to solve problems.
   b. Don't fix blame or point fingers.
   c. Show how action leads to a higher skill level.
   d. Clearly reinforce expectations.
   e. Develop action plans and practice follow-up.
   f. Don't put down person for past mistakes.
   g. Spend more time on discussing future improvements and less time on the past incident.

5. **ACCENTUATE THAT THE TEAMMATE WILL SEE POSITIVE RESULTS FROM CHANGING BEHAVIOR.**
   a. This change will make you more proficient, more valuable, more competent.
   b. Will help grow one's self-esteem.
   c. Develops teamwork.
   d. Makes the company more profitable.
   e. Develops self-motivation.
   f. Develops trust.
   g. Show how everyone wins with the improvement (person, department, company).

6. **DO NOT WAIT UNTIL THE ANNUAL PERFORMANCE APPRAISAL PROCESS TO DELIVER CRITICISM.**
   a. By the time the performance appraisal comes around, there should be no surprises.
   b. Inform individual how this (action) is being recorded.
   c. Provide a person a known opportunity is available to them to improve in a specific area before evaluation time.
   d. Praising should be done a lot.
   e. Confront issues on a timely basis.
   f. Time until review is wasted and company performance is poorer if you wait.
   g. Person should be given a chance to show improvement before annual review. Don't let a person lose a wage increase because of a lack of timely feedback.

7. **CLARIFY THE CONSEQUENCES OF NOT CORRECTING BEHAVIOR.**
   a. Explain what this action, or lack of it, means to the company and to the individual.
   b. Make sure you follow through or your creditability is lost.
   c. Don't be overly tolerable on allowing individuals not to follow rules (e.g. absenteeism, lateness).
   d. Explain disciplinary actions.
   e. Lay out specifics of consequences.

The Magic Workbook, Michigan State University Press, 1999

Role-Playing Exercise

Identify at least two actual situations that are not adequately, if at all, being addressed by management at this time. Please provide as much detail as possible.

Identify at least two actual situations that are addressed over and over with no lasting solution ever seeming to be achieved.

CRITICISM/DISCIPLINE

SESSION # 3

A brief review of sessions # 1 & 2 is done during the first ten to fifteen minutes and then an additional ten to fifteen minutes of new culture ideas are introduced. Participants then share their role-playing examples. This usually leads to a lively dialogue as to how to best frame or explain the organization's unsolved problems or personnel conflicts. These examples are recorded and used throughout the balance of the sessions.

The balance of the time in this session is devoted to having two individuals role-play a situation for the group. We try to use a problem identified from the homework. However, we are prepared with a standard role-playing scenario such as excessive absenteeism or an individual extending breaks and lunchtimes. After the presentation everyone in the class is required to share what they liked and would have changed if they were participating in the role-playing scene. This starts to help form the culture change on how the organization will modify its current ways of trying to solve problems. The ideas of the group regarding how the role-playing could have been improved are recorded and presented to them in a handout as a "memory jogger" at the start of session # 4. (See an example of a **"Memory Jogger"**)

The sandwich approach for how to approach a conflict-solving session is explained. Participants are told that a sincere compliment should be stated in the beginning, followed by the meat (conflict) in the middle with another piece of bread (a compliment or something positive said) to wrap things up. This is the first of three approaches to how to structure a conflict session to be shared with the group. Participants are informed that they have to choose which structure or combination of ideas to use when dealing with conflicts.

Participants are encouraged to submit additional role-playing scenarios that the organization needs to address or improve. The homework assigned for session # 4 is to identify the type of environment they would like to work in to grow people.

(See **Session # 3 – Homework**) Once again they are paired with someone who they have not worked with previously to do the homework.

DISCIPLINE

Homework # 3

CREATING A PROPER ENVIRONMENT

WHAT ARE SOME ASPECTS OF A PROPER CULTURE (ENVIRONMENT) THAT ENABLE A MANAGER TO DELIVER EFFECTIVE CRITICISM?

WHAT HAS TO BE DONE AT YOUR ORGANIZATION TO CREATE THIS TYPE OF A CULTURE?

CRITICISM/DISCIPLINE

SESSION # 4

A brief review of prior sessions occupies the first fifteen minutes. Participants then share what they discussed and concluded regarding session # 3's homework. Their preferred work environment is recorded and a typed summary is given to them at the start of session # 5. There is a lively discussion of what should be versus what is.

Two additional role-playing scenarios are done. These two scenarios are taken directly from the list that the group has presented. We usually try to reverse the responsibility of the two participants. For example, a foreperson would play the plant manager while the plant manager would play the worker having a conflict with the foreperson.

All participants provide what they liked and would change if they were an active participant in the scene. Any new suggestions are added to the "memory jogger" list and a revised list is given to them as a handout at the start of session # 5.

The second concept for how to approach a conflict is presented to the group. (See the handout of "**Empathy Communication**.")

At the start of the class everyone is told that we will give hugs before we adjourn. A lot of interesting comments are made. About fifteen minutes before the ending time, "verbal hugs" are introduced to the group. Each person is required to send and receive at least one positive compliment. The purpose of this is to teach them to become comfortable with complimenting each other. Our experience indicates that most participants by this time feel very comfortable complementing other participants. This will be the procedure that we will use to close the balance of the meetings.

Homework due for session # 5 is assigned on "Crucial Hiring Questions." (See handout on **Crucial Prehire Questions** and **Homework # 4**.)

DISCIPLINE

Empathy Communication

Paraphrasing & Reflecting Feelings

⊗ How is it going with that particular problem?

⊗ How do you feel about that?

⊗ How would you like it to be?

⊗ What will have to happen to make it better?

⊗ Do you have a plan?

⊗ Is there some way I can be of help?

DISCIPLINE
Homework # 4

Crucial Prehire Questions

- Tell me about the best manager you've worked for. Why was he or she such a good manager? What would your ideal boss be like?

- What was your least favorite manager like? How did you handle the things you didn't like about him or her?

- Tell me about a disagreement you and a previous boss had. How did you resolve it?

- What kind of direction and feedback is most helpful to you? Do you prefer to work independently or with lots of guidance?

- If I became your boss, what would be the most important thing for me to say or do to support you?

CRITICISM/DISCIPLINE

SESSION # 5

A fifteen-minute review period of insights and learning from the prior session is recorded and discussed. The homework from session # 4 on "Crucial Prehire Questions" ensues. There is a lively dialogue on what the organization should be doing. It provides an inside look at the type of teammates they wish to grow with in the future.

Two additional role-playing scenarios are played through by individuals who have not done a role-playing scenario up to this session. Role-playing actual organizational situations is usually well received and is beneficial to all participants.

The third method for how one might approach a conflict opportunity is presented. We refer to it as the DASR approach. The three basic guidelines for sending criticism under this approach are: first, **Set Realistic Goals and Expectations**; Second, **Be Immediate** with your action; and third, **Be Specific** by using **DASR**. (**Describe, Acknowledge, Specify,** and **Reaffirm** your script regarding the conflict.) [See **handout** for these **Guidelines For Sending Criticism**.]

Participants are told that they usually will blend the sandwich, empathy, and DASR methods for confronting conflicts. They can also follow any one they deem appropriate for the specific situation. This is the last of the three methods presented to the group. During sessions 6, 7, and 8 the group will be asked to identify which method the management role-players use. This is a reinforcement for learning the methods.

Verbal hugs (compliments) are sent and received by everyone.

Homework for session # 6 will be the most sensitive one the group will have to face. By this time a good bonding or team-building spirit has developed. Session # 6 homework requires the random pairing to identify the person whom they are having the greatest challenge in getting along with at the organization. **(See Session # 5 – Homework)**

Remember to pair up different individuals for each different homework assignment. This provides an opportunity for everyone to work together. This, in turn, usually provides the two individuals with better understanding of one another. This is usually a positive building block for future cooperation and understanding.

SOME PRESENTATION MEMORY JOGGERS:

Who has **_control_** of the situation?

Good or poor **_eye contact_**?

Do you feel that **_sufficient_** praise was given?

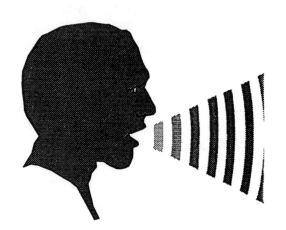

Did you come to the **_specific point_** of the meeting?

Had you **_collected_** enough facts, data, times, places and people involved to support your specific point?

Did you adequately **_present_** the collection of facts, data and so forth?

Was your body language and posture **_neutral_**?

Did you end with a **_plan_** *for* corrective behavior? Who initiated the **_first version_** of the correction plan?

Did you establish a **_time line_** to review the progress and the possible need to adjust the plan?

Where did you meet **_privately or publicly_**?

Did you consult one of your **_colleagues_** as a sounding board?

Guidelines for Giving Criticism

Step # 1:

Set Realistic Goals and Expectations

Step # 2:

Be Immediate

Step # 3:

Be Specific [DASR] (Describe, Acknowledge, Specify and Reaffirm script)

DISCIPLINE
Homework # 5

ENERGY VAMPIRE EXERCISES

1. Identify the person in the organization whom you are having the most challenging time dealing with at this time.

2. Describe to your exercise partner the nature and history of this uncomfortable challenge.

3. Discuss with your partner what new approaches you are planning to use to improve this situation.

4. Establish a date by which this will be accomplished.

The Magic Workbook, Michigan State University Press, 1999

CRITICISM/DISCIPLINE

SESSION # 6

Insights and learning since our last meeting are discussed for about fifteen minutes. Many times examples of how some of the prior learning has been used is shared.

First we identify what an energy vampire, "dream killer," or "bad apple" means to the group. This list is recorded and then given to the group as a handout at the next meeting. (See **Handout** on some "**Energy Vampire**" definitions)

Next everyone identifies who their particular "energy vampire" is. Sometimes it is someone in the group. Whether the "energy vampire" is someone in the group or not, there is a healthy discussion of what might be done to help grow the relationship. It takes a lot of courage and trust for this to happen. It is a continuation of team building and growing people.

Next, two more role-playing sessions are done. As with all of them, everyone shares their opinion of what was good and what they would have changed if they were playing the manager's role. Almost all role-playing sessions bring a lively discussion of the facts and how to handle the situation.

Verbal hugs are shared at the end of the meeting.

Homework for the last two sessions are specific role-playing scenarios for specific individuals. Once again new teams of two are paired and told to prepare a real organizational situation for another specific team to role-play. The team preparing the role-play scenario will specify which member of the other team will be the manager having to confront the conflict. Randomly the two teams that will be exchanging role-playing situations are identified. Each team knows to whom they are going to have role-play their scenario. Some of the individuals will be having their second opportunity to role-play.

"BAD APPLES"

"ENERGY VAMPIRES"

"DREAM KILLERS"

1. People who whine and complain.

2. People who don't give a full day's work.

3. People who watch the clock.

4. People who are unwilling to learn.

5. People who are nonproductive.

6. People who say one thing and do another.

7. People who put their personal ambitions above the welfare of the rest.

8. People who don't care.

9. People who aren't happy to be employed at your organization.

10. People who don't work at a decent pace.

11. People who watch other people instead of focusing on their own work.

12. People who have a "me" first rather than a "we" attitude.

CRITICISM/DISCIPLINE

SESSION # 7

Insights and learning are shared. Then one team is selected to present to the other the role-playing scenario they will have to play out for the group. The usual feedback and reinforcement of things to do and not to do is done after each presentation.

Depending on the group and how things are progressing, sometimes the specific role-playing scenarios are given to the participants before the meeting so that they have time to anticipate and prepare for their role-playing opportunity. It has been our experience that if each participant does one role-play without any time to prepare and one with time to prepare more is gained. You can see what one can do on the spot with conflicts and what one can do with some time to think about it.

All participants increase their self-confidence and comfort level through these role-playing situations. They now have been given some methodology as to how to deal with conflict. Another big benefit is that they have bonded with their colleagues in facing discipline issues. A camaraderie develops in this group because of the common tasks and role-playing exercises that they have been required to do.

Meeting is adjourned with the usual verbal hugs. These verbal hugs are teaching people how to grow themselves as well as others. The more you do it, the easier it is, and the more you think of doing it.

CRITICISM/DISCIPLINE

SESSION # 8

Insights and learning from the prior session are discussed.

Role-playing scenarios are completed with the usual feedback after each team completes its part. The role-playing continues to improve with each new presentation. By this time almost all role-players are comfortable and doing a good job in dealing with the situations given to them. Not only is the group becoming comfortable and improved with handling conflicts, but after doing so much realistic role-playing, they have new ideas, support and confidence as to how to deal with real issues outside the learning center.

The last thirty minutes or so are used to go around the table and have each participant share what they have learned from the eight sessions. It is one last time for each person to subliminally tune themselves into their new ways of dealing with conflict, but it also reinforces for the group how much everyone has improved. It is a confidence builder as well as one last way for everyone to learn and share with each other.

The session ends with verbal hugs.

Our experience has been that every group would like to continue on with more sessions on how to grow themselves and deal with issues. We have provided them with additional sessions, not only to reinforce what they have already learned, but also expand their awareness of how to accomplish more.

WORLD-CLASS IDEAS

When it comes to continual improvement, everyone must be involved. Ideas for improvement coming from only a few people will result in only a few improvements. Good companies in Japan implement over one hundred ideas per associate per year. We have not done that well, but we now implement twelve ideas per associate per year, twenty times better than the average U.S. company.

We believe that the traditional suggestion box approach is not that effective. Many times unsigned suggestions are not fully explained, yet there is no way to contact those making the suggestions. This format is also impersonal and momentum usually dies out quickly. An idea is worth nothing unless it is implemented. In our system, the lead person closest to the change approves the idea for the sake of avoiding counterproductive actions. Taking pictures of the changes and posting them helps others see that change is occurring and stimulates ideas for their own work areas. A small monetary recognition is awarded, by random drawing among those making suggestions, after each fifteen implemented ideas. Each employee and mini-company (see chapter 9) have a set annual goal for the number of implemented ideas.

Everyone seems to be looking for the immediate and big payoff. That is not reality. The team should be rewarded only after real changes happen. It is our belief that a system of many small changes (KAIZEN) is the way to go. We all would like the large savings that one blockbuster idea could bring, but there are not that many of these out there that each individual can achieve. Consequently, we believe that a continuing program of many small changes instills the desire and appreciation for change in the culture, promotes an understanding of teamwork, and allows the organization to continually reduce costs.

WORLD–CLASS IDEAS 1998

Implemented ideas are a key source of continuous improvement by having all our associates involved. Eliminating waste and adding value for our internal and external customers will be the driving force.

We will still have a drawing after fifteen implemented ideas. First $25/Second $15/Third $10 - Total $50.

NEW PROGRAM FOR 1998

Goal of 12 implemented ideas per associate. (See below for eligibility.)

A.   Pay $3.00 for every implemented idea at year-end.

B.   Pay $1.00 to the Pot for each implemented idea for a drawing at year-end.
Pot (5 Winners)   30% 1st Name • 25% 2nd Name • 20% 3rd Name
15% 4th Name • 10% 5th Name

NOTE: Payout A. and B. above at fiscal year-end Christmas Party.

RULES

1.   Every associate must have twelve implemented ideas. If not, the associate is not eligible for Pot drawing.
2.   Each mini-company must hit 80% of Goal (twelve implemented ideas per associate). If not, no one in the mini-company is eligible for Pot Drawing.
3.   Your name will be placed in Pot Drawing when you reach twelve implemented ideas and your mini-company hits 80% of goal.
4.   Every idea earns $3.00 and $1.00 for the Pot - even if five or ten associates work on one idea (split $3.00).
5.   The person or persons with the idea get the $3.00, but they could share with the implementor.
6.   Each idea should show the area of improvement - Quality, Cost, Delivery, Safety, Morale.
7.   Limit of $5,000 total for individual and Pot - Does not include regular drawing after fifteen ideas.
8.   Leads will determine if the idea qualifies.
9.   Each person who qualifies for the final drawing will have one chance to win.
10.   WORLD-CLASS IDEA BOARD
The establishment of the World-Class Idea Board is to encourage associate suggestions on how to journey forward in our efforts to continually improve. The procedure is as follows:

1.   All departments have the ability, and are encouraged, to input all implemented ideas into the external program of the Powerway Menu.
2.   All ideas will be presented at the Weekly Lead Meeting by one of the people attending.
3.   All ideas must be fully implemented and not just a suggestion.
4.   All ideas must help MAGIC move toward its goal. ("To make money now and in the future.")
5.   A picture and write-up of the idea, individual, or individuals will be posted on the World-Class Idea Board.
6.   After every fifteen implemented suggestions submitted at the weekly Lead Meeting, a drawing will be held for three (3) winners. ($25, $15, $10). Any idea has an equal chance to win.
7.   The randomly drawn idea will be posted on the Culture Board.

MAGIC INC.

VISITOR NOTIFICATION

DATE of visit: _____

DAY of week: _____

TIME of visit: _____ - _____

TOTAL NUMBER of visitors: _____

☐ CUSTOMER

☐ CO MPETITOR

☐ SUPPLIER

☐ OTHER_____

DISTRIBUTION LIST _____
_____
_____ _____
_____ _____
_____ _____
_____ _____
_____ _____
_____ _____
_____ _____
_____ _____

NAMES	TITLES	COMPANY

FOCUS OF VISIT: _____

_____

- IS SUPPORT OF OTHERS REQUIRED?_____ WHO?_____
- WHAT AREAS WILL BE TOURED?_____
- WHAT CONFERENCE ROOM HAS BEEN RESERVED? _____
- IS LUNCH OR OTHER REFRESHMENT REQUIRED?_____
- WHO IS RESPONSIBLE FOR THIS TASK (lunch, etc)? _____

COMMENTS: _____

REMEMBER:
1. SAFETY GLASSES (ear protection optional)
2. ASK FOR FEEDBACK/DOCUMENT
3. KPI'S (Q,C,D,S,M)
4. VIDEO
5. PLACE NAME ON MONITOR (give to front office)

PERSON SETTING UP TOUR
(Please print your name)

MAGIC, INC.

138 ERIE ST, CHICAGO IL 60671 • (630) 555-4491 fax (630) 555-0951

Supplier Performance Report
June, 1998

11111

BOULDER PRODUCTS
743 LAKE DRIVE

CHICAGO, IL 60671

OVERALL PERFORMANCE	
Possible Pts This Month:	100.00
Deductions This Month:	7.00
Total Points This Month:	**107.00**
12 Month Average:	**104.83**
Current Status:	**Certified**

History	1	2	3	4	5	6	7	8	9	10	11	12	Pct	Avg
Quality	40.00	40.00	40.00	40.00	40.00	40.00	40.00	40.00	40.00	40.00	40.00	40.00	100.00%	40.00
Service	25.00	26.00	27.00	26.00	29.00	28.00	28.00	27.00	28.00	25.00	27.00	26.00	107.33%	26.83
Delivery	37.00	37.00	38.00	39.00	38.00	39.00	40.00	37.00	37.00	38.00	38.00	38.00	108.57%	38.00

	1	2	3	4	5	6	7	8	9	10	11	12	Pct
Totals:	102.00	103.00	105.00	105.00	107.00	107.00	108.00	104.00	105.00	103.00	105.00	104.00	104.83%

QUALITY PERFORMANCE

Start with 40 Points. A deduction of 5 Points is made for each SDMR issued.

Maximum Points:	**40**
Deductions:	**0**
Total:	**40**

SERVICE PERFORMANCE

Start with 25 Points. A deduction of 1 Point is made for each occurrence in the 4 performance categories shown below.

Improper Paperwork
Packaging
Communications
Supplier Commitment
Exceptional Service   3

Maximum Points:	**25**
Points:	**3**
Total:	**28**

DELIVERY PERFORMANCE

Start with 35 Points. A deduction of 1 Point is made for each late delivery. Add 1 Point for each exceptional delivery. Requirement is 100% on-time delivery.

Maximum Points:	**35**
Late Shipment	
Exceptional Delivery	**4**
Total:	**39**

Issued By:

Quality Manager

Material Manager

SQA Manager

The Magic Workbook, Michigan State University Press, 1999

ORIENTATION

Good people will make you a good company. We start the process of finding good people by our hiring and orientation processes. After the basic screening process of a completed application form, we decide whom to invite in for an interview. Three senior managers interview each candidate. Once a candidate is considered a possible fit for our culture, they are interviewed by people from the mini-company that the candidate will be assigned to. It may take twenty candidates to find that one associate who we feel will help us grow. We believe in spending time in the front end choosing a person rather than spending a lot of time to get an individual to change while on the job.

During a new associate's first couple of weeks on the job, they attend a two-day orientation program. (See attachments.) Each manager spends time sharing who they are and what they do as well as answering questions. One day lunch is shared with all the managers, and the next day lunch is shared with someone from each focus group. We are trying to make new associates feel comfortable and to introduce them to who is who as well as to help them appreciate our positive culture.

After the two-day orientation new associates attend a 15-week, two and a half hour, in-house class on quality and related issues. (See attachments.) Everyone is tested as to their comprehension of the materials. Associates cannot work at a job without the required knowledge. A mentor is assigned to each associate for at least six months. All mentors go through a mentoring training program. They must retake any class they fail. Every fifteen weeks, the class cycle starts anew. This allows associates who need to retake a class to do so, and it permits everybody to refresh their knowledge of the content. These classes are also open to our suppliers.

MAGIC, INC.
Indoctrination for New Employees

Day ONE **MARCH 19, 1998**

	start	finish	duration	Subject	Instructor	instructors initials
1	8:30	9:00	30 minutes	New Employee Introduction	Verna Coburn+	_____
2	9:00	10:15	75 minutes	Review Handbook	Mike Langly	_____
3	10:15	10:25	10 minutes	Break		
4	10:25	11:10	45 minutes	Vision, Mission, Action	Mike L, Rod B, Peter T	_____
5	11:10	12:00	50 minutes	Safety	Mike Dillion	_____
6	12:00	1:00	60 minutes	Lunch w/Leads & Staff		_____
7	1:00	2:15	75 minutes	Quality & tagging, traceability	Alan Cooper / Mike Thomas	_____
8	2:15	2:25	10 minutes	Break		
9	2:25	2:55	30 minutes	Customer Focus	Rod Berman	_____
10	2:55	3:45	50 minutes	Lou Holtz Video Tape	Verna Coburn	_____
		total	435 minutes			

Day TWO

	start	finish	duration	Subject	Instructor	instructors initials
1	10:00	11:00	60 minutes	Benefits Enrollment	Pam Townsen+	_____
2	11:00	12:00	60 minutes	SPC	Linda Williams	_____
3	12:00	12:40	40 minutes	Lunch w/Committee Representatives, QA Resource, & Mentors	Workplace Org, Culture, Safety, Preventive Maint, Setup Reduction	_____
4	12:40	1:40	60 minutes	SPC	Linda Williams	_____
5	1:40	2:20	40 minutes	Paradigm Video Tape	Pam Townsen	_____
6	2:20	2:30	10 minutes	Break		
7	2:30	2:50	20 minutes	Feedback & Questions	ML, RB, PT, Lead	
8	2:50	3:30	40 minutes	Bob Mowad Video Tape	Verna Coburn +	
		total	350 minutes			

+ may substitute other qualified MAGIC Associate

I have completed the above 16 hours of indoctrination. _____

                                                  signature   date

INDOCTRINATION OUTLINE
Peter T., Rod B., or Mike L.

REVIEW VISION
"BEST AT WHAT WE DO"
a) The importance of being the best
b) Competing in world market
c) What our customers expect
d) Why they expect this
e) Continuous improve
f) Elimination of waste

MISSION
"Profits through Quality and have fun during the process"
a) Four Stakeholders
b) Q C D S M
c) KPI Boards (attached)
d) Mini-Co. - How they operate

ACTION PLAN
a) Education
b) Robust Process
c) Customer Focus
d) TQM - Improvement
e) Celebration

FIVE PLUS TWO FOCUS

5

a) IPMP - Control of Poor Material
b) HOUSEKEEPING - Everything in place
c) SAFE ENVIRONMENT
d) ORGANIZED EFFICIENT
e) PREVENTIVE MAINTENANCE - Equipment in good running condition
f) SAMPLE BOARD - Help prevent mistakes
g) SET-UP TASK FORCE -Fourslide department trying to reduce set-up time

+2

TOTAL QUALITY MANAGEMENT - Quality throughout the complete organization.
Continual improvements and elimination of waste.

CULTURE - Creating a culture for MAGIC - Enjoy working with others as a team to reach our goal. "Profits through Quality" and have fun doing it.

HISTORY BOARD

FOCUS GROUPS -

REVIEW CULTURE BOOKLET

Announcing

There will be indoctrination for:.BOB FREEMAN, TR: BRIAN SUTTON, PR: FRED BOLDER, VA: TRICIA LIGHTS, VA.

Indoctrination will be held on <u>THURSDAY, 12/17/98</u> AND <u>FRIDAY 12/18/98</u>

Please refer to the attached schedule for the time and day you are scheduled for your part in indoctrination.

Let's give these new folks a nice warm welcome to MAGIC, INC!

To;

WHO	Assignment (in addition to instructor commitments on the attached schedule)
Mike Langly	lunch day one
Rod Bernan	lunch day one
Michael Dillion	facilitate lunch day two
Alan Cooper	notify QA Resource, lunch day one
QA Resource(s)	lunch day two
Peter Thompson	lunch day one
Mike Thomas	lunch day one
Donna Weederman	lunch day one
Lonnie Courtwite	lunch day one
Patrick Lever	appoint Culture Committe Rep for lunch day two
Wade Parker	lunch day one
Dan Sheldon	lunch day one
Rose Dannon	lunch day one
Verna Coburn	order lunches, lunch day one
Linda Williams	lunch day two
Dale Cooper	lunch day one
Mentors	lunch day two
Mike Sanders	WPO Committee Rep for lunch day two
Craig Horton	lunch day one
Dan Jacks	lunch day one
Rod Sands	lunch day two
Pam Townsen	lunch day two
Ed Fields	lunch day one

The Magic Workbook, Michigan State University Press, 1999

KEY VALUES

1. Customer Focus: to bring delight from our services. Our goal is to form partnerships by giving our customers:

    - Zero parts per million defects (PPM)
    - 100% On-time delivery
    - Competitive prices when looking at total cost
    - Timely and innovative service, beyond their expectations
    - Timely and proactive communications
    - Design support

We will continue to monitor Quality, Cost, Delivery, and Service using both formal and informal systems to measure our effectiveness. Innovation and technology sharing will be tools that will help MAGIC reach our Goal.

2. Associate Focus:

A) <u>T R I C</u>

TRUST	Character and competence at all levels of organization.
RELATIONSHIP	All associates feel part of **MAGIC** family, understanding their part to contribute to the team for improvement. Consideration for each other, customers, suppliers, and community.
INTEGRITY	Honest, trustworthy, "Walk the Talk."
COMMUNICATION	Every associate knows where we/they are going and why. All necessary information is communicated on a timely basis.

B) All associates are involved to make decisions. They are expected to take ownership of the company's goals.

MAGIC, INC.

Ongoing Quality Training

1/5/98

to:

instructors,	students,	Rose Dannon,	Dale Cooper
Donna W.,	Mike Langly,	Mike Dillion	Rod Berman
Alan Cooper	Verna Coburn	Christine A.	Ed Fields

from: Pam Townsen

Status of current ongoing quality training sessions.
Wednesdays 9:00 -11:00 or 3:00 - 5:00
(whichever fits your schedule)

CLASSES ARE HELD IN THE UPSTAIRS CLASSROOM

Week		Date	Subject	Instructor	Where
1	**	10/15/97	Math	Dan Sheldon	classroom
2	**	10/22/97	Math	Dan Sheldon	classroom
3		10/29/97	Blueprint Reading	Michael Sanders	classroom
4		11/05/97	Calipers/Micrometer/Height Gage	John Timber	classroom
5	**	11/12/97	Comparator	Alan Cooper	final audit area
6	*	11/19/97	SPC introduction	Linda Williams	classroom
8	**	11/26/97	PowerWay Operations	Linda Williams	classroom
9		12/03/97	SPC capability w/hands on	Linda Williams	classroom
10		12/10/97	Control charts as a tool - analysis	Linda Williams	classroom
11		12/17/97	Control chart analysis cont.	Linda Williams	classroom
		12/24/97	no class		
		12/31/97	no class		
12		01/07/97	Control charts + process analysis	Linda Williams	classroom
13	*	01/15/97	Problem Solving Tools	Mike Langly	classroom
14		01/22/97	Quality is more than SPC	Linda Williams	classroom
15	**	01/29/97	PowerWay Document Manager	Linda Williams	classroom
16		02/05/97	SPC Review	Linda Williams	classroom
17	**	02/12/97	SPC Test	Linda Williams	classroom

** - skills chart item

 * - required by everyone

All classes are open to anyone - **please let me know** ahead of time **of additional students**. Also please let me **know if there is anyone missing from this list.**

current students are;

other students	problem solving class only	new students
		Deb Karpter (qa)
Michael Kamp (tr) finish	Harland Helman (mtl ctl)	Vicki Darger (pr)
Ron Putter (tr) finish	Karen Low (office)	Matt Middleton (eng)
John Langly (tr) finish	Rod Berman (office)	Peter Landon (eng)
Mark Robins (tr) finish	Jan Landers (office)	Hien Little (va)
Shannon Planters (pr) ????	Anne Brandon (mtl ctl)	Kevin Stame (tr)
		Josh Omer (fs)
	Ed Shullert (mtl ctl)	Ed Fields (fs)
	Pam Townsen (office)	Jonathan Yoders (st)
		Manh Little (fs)
Mary Brittle - review and test only		Angelica Jordon (va)
		Linda McMillian (va)

The Magic Workbook, Michigan State University Press, 1999

SPC/Quality Education Outline

Class #1
Calipers / Micrometer / Height Gage
- detailed guidelines for proper usage

Class #2
Comparator
- polar and cartesian coordinates
- metric and english conversion
- incremental measurements
- radius and diameter measurements and conversions
- finding center locations
- center of radius to center of radius measurements
- measuring angles , finding complimentary angles
- finding the vertex
- using memory function (storing, recalling, finding measurement between memory locations and clearing memory)
- midpoint between two points

Class #3
Math
- addition and subtraction with positive and negative numbers
- multiplication
- division
- M.D.A.S. (My Dear Aunt Sally)

Class #4
Math
- fractions
- converting fractions to decimals
- percentages
- converting english to metric
- averages
- equations

Class #5
Variation
- definition of variation, everything varies
- collect data (roll dice)
- discuss data
- make histogram from data
- discuss different view of the same data (as a picture)
- apply curve to histogram
- normal curve (predictable pattern)
- how discussion applies to job (compare measuring 100% to taking samples and making predictions and how?)
- introduce sigma and the percentages of a normal distribution
- introduce terms

Variation continued
- less or more variation?
- different shapes of normal curve
- causes of variation (common causes , special causes — examples and effect of on normal curve)
- type of variation (within piece, piece to piece, time to time)

Detection/Prevention
- introduce the detection model
- play through scenario of suppliers and customers with initial supplier of poor quality.
- introduce the prevention model

- discuss differences (points..can't inspect quality in - and no matter how much checking is done the parts aren't going to be any better)
- recap main points and answer any remaining questions

SPC

- SPC concept originally developed with this theory to monitor the process - 'The quality (consistency, robustness) of the process determines the quality (consistency, variation) of the product. Therefore by measuring the quality (results of process, specific characteristics) of the product we determine the quality (consistency, robustness) of the process.'
- SPC is a manufacturing tool used to monitor common causes and detect special causes.
- SPC is a tool, not the goal (tool for the process not goal of the process)

NEXT CLASS BRING CALIPERS

Class #6
Control Charts

- two types of data (attribute and variable)
- control charts; characteristics of, types of, examples of, when/what different types used for
- purpose of - monitor common causes, detect special causes, 'control charts help us (statistically) compare the current process output to previous output in effort to detect any changes out of the ordinary, within the process
- go over areas of attribute charts; graphs, info, data (what's a subgroup)
- attribute test with SR parts and slip through gage, discuss probability
- go over areas of variable charts
- go over steps of data collection (including how to collect samples)
- hands-on variable chart exercise (measure, record, and plot points nine subgroups)
- about control limits

Class #7
PowerWay Operations (hands-on using computers in the classroom)

- screens
- keystrokes
- sessions (subsessions, master sessions)
- open session, enter data,
- measurement error procedure (practice)
- practice
- entering comments
- first pc program

PowerWay Operations continued

- ccs database
- document manager, introduction to
- do change setup (changing MI#)
- close session
- control limits in PowerWay

NEXT CLASS BRING CALIPERS

Class #8
Capability

- review terms
- review normal curve (result of common cause variation)
- what is capability (apply specs to curve)
- Cpk, cp, cr
- where do we use
- how is data collected
- what is needed (30 pcs min., only common causes)
- hands-on capability study (30 pc study)

- cp and cr only relationship, Cpk deals with location
- cp is best Cpk can be (with current distribution centered)
- show examples of curves and specs - what do we do to correct/improve (i.e. center process, reduce common cause variation, nothing, center and reduce variation)
- goalpost mentality vs Taguichi loss function
- show where related information is in PowerWay

Class #9
Control Charts / SPC
- Video Q#3 - Perry Johnson

Class #10
Control Charts - Analysis
- Video - SPC #4 - Chart Interpretation
- what is out-of control (special cause = something out of ordinary = something is changing in process, one of the 5 common causes)
- know your process - must be able to apply SPC concept to your process - the chart is a tool to tell you if something is changing. Know what point in the process is affecting the outcome of the characteristic that is being measured. It's all cause and effect (for every action there is an equal and opposite reaction) map out the flow of the process - fix the root cause instead of compensating for the change somewhere else in the process - fix the cause not the effect.
- patterns and points beyond control limits are considered 'not normal' because (based on past performance data) their occurrence is not probable. Like when rolling dice it isn't likely that you roll pair of ones followed by pair of twos then pair of threes, etc. - it just isn't likely to happen without something special/something different going on - something is causing it.
- stratification - is either positive special cause or fudging - what are the effects of fudging and why do some people think they need to make the numbers look 'good'
- three answers that must be documented for any out-of-control situation (cause, correction, disposition)
- GRS&S procedure for responding to out-of-control (first remeasure and eliminate self as special cause— i.e., measurement error)
- just because the screen doesn't turn red or point isn't beyond the control limit doesn't mean that everything is 'normal' - we must look at the chart and take note of any sudden shifts or visible changes

Control Charts - Analysis continued
- the range graph is more sensitive, you can be right on target yet have increased variation significantly. If you only look at the average you are only reading half the story. (the average and range graph combined create a curve)
- SPC isn't meant to be a permanent check - it is meant to eliminate itself through improvement in the process - refinement of common causes and elimination of possible special causes (equate to kid and homework - in the 5th grade it's bug bug bug, check check check, by 9th grade homework should be taken care of without bugging and checking - it's an automatic) if not total elimination then at least reduction in frequency (every 30 minutes to every 2 hours to every shift to...)

Class #11
Control Charts - Analysis
- characteristics being charted need to be important to the customer or important to our process (it's a waste of time to chart a characteristic that doesn't relate to key variables in the process)
- a picture is worth 1,000 words, but every picture tells 1,000 stories - comments are the key to interpreting the story that the graph (control chart) tells.
- when making comments you must answer all three questions —'no adj' is not acceptable
- in comments, if noting that adjustment was made then specify what was adjusted and in what direction
- terminology can be important - remember average = mean ≠ target. So if you intend to say that the process is running at the target, - say that, - but don't say parts are running at mean (the parts are and will always run at a mean value)
- if a special cause occurs and is then accepted into the process (i.e. new coil of material parts are still well within spec and capable) then don't allow the control chart to continuously exhibit an out-of-control situation. Adjust the chart to fit the new process - repeat - if a special cause is introduced

and accepted then the process has changed and requires new control limits in order to reflect the new process
- affect of overadjustment - we don't want to constantly adjust - adjusting is a waste of time - we want the process to be robust and to run on it's own. Also, overadjustment adds variation to the product.
- use proper tool for job - there are different control charts for different types of variation. (you wouldn't want to carry a bowling ball in a paper sack)
- difference between in control and within specification

Class #12
Problem-Solving Tools
- Plan - Do - Study - Act Cycle   (system improvement, the people principle, the knowledge principle, planned change principle)
- Brainstorming (task and purpose, structured/unstructured, guidelines/rules, example/exercise)
- Pareto (history - 80/20 rule, description, example, summary)
- Cause and Effect (definition, form construction and examples)

Class #13
Quality Is More Than SPC
- review of detection vs prevention
- discuss sorting/rework - not 100% effective - do the find the 'f' activity (100% sorting only 80% effective). Quality must be built into the process - you can't inspect quality into the parts/product
- history of SPC, leaders in quality; Juran - Deming - Crosby
- Deming's forteen points

Quality Is More Than SPC continued

- who's responsible for quality
- what is the purpose of a quality system (CI, kaizen, poke yoke, standardization, long-term thinking, SOP, reoccurrence prevention) - how do you know exercise and be careful what you ask for example
- cost of quality (prevention, appraisal , internal failure, external failure)
- quality and KPI indicators at GRS&S (ref. quality manual, how it relates to bottom line - gainsharing!)
- quality as a 'career' - about ASQC and certifications and membership, about GRCC classes.
- quality awards (Baldridge, Deming, A.R. Hedberg through PMA)

Class #14
PowerWay Document Manager
- comment logs
- quality alerts
- inspection instructions
- Alt-F2
- F2
- external programs
- editing criteria

Class #15
Test

MINI-COMPANIES
(SELF - DIRECTED)

Develop Mission and Business Plan
Prepare needs assessment
Plan to accomplish improvements in QCDSM
Annual trade shows
Monthly network with all leads
Daily huddles, weekly meetings review progess
Monthly progress meeting

FOCUS GROUPS

GROUP	LEAD	NUMBER	TIME
COMPUTER VISION	LINDA WILLIAMS	5	MONTHLY
CULTURE	ROD BERMAN/VERNA COBURN	6	MONTHLY
WORK PLACE ORGANIZATION (WPO)	MICHAEL SANDERS	5	MONTHLY
MINI-COMPANY	FS, ST, PR, MC/RES, AD/RES	ALL EMP	WEEKLY
OFFICERS	BY MINI - CO	3	WEEKLY
OFFICERS	BY MAGIC	12	WEEKLY
BANKERS OFFICERS	ROD B/MIKE L/PETER T, ALAN C, MIKE D -	6	MONTHLY
MATERIAL REVIEW BOARD (MRB)	ROD BERMAN	5+QA REPS	WEEKLY
FS CIUG	TOM WARNER	4	MONTHLY
MACHINE AWARENESS COMMITTEE (MAC)	BEN JONES	7	MONTHLY
ISO9002/QS9000	ALAN COOPER	8	WEEKLY
ROBUST PROCESS	MIKE DILLON	7	WEEKLY
SAFETY	MIKE DILLON	6	MONTHLY
TRAINING DEVELOPEMENT	MIKE LANGLY	9	WEEKLY
SPP	ROB BERMAN	6	QUARTERLY
STRATEGIC PLANNING	ROD BERMAN	10	QUARTERLY

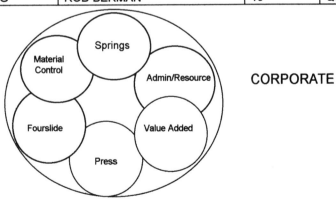 CORPORATE

All mini-companies operate within the corporate framework and plan their missions to help meet corporate objectives. Six mini-companies all learn from each other (network and sharing.). Independent, yet all working within the overall framework.

Lifelong Education

There is a mind shift occurring in this country to the belief that employers will be the primary educators in the next century. We believe that it is imperative that an organization continuously grow its associates. It is a shame that so many companies have no formal education programs. We decided that to insure the future of Magic, we had to guarantee the intellectual growth of all associates.

Some ideas and actions we have tried:

- At least every other week, every one of our associates attends a one-hour class. Each class is videotaped for those who cannot attend. The life-long education topics are divided between 75 percent business-related topics and 25 percent personal, social, and spiritual growth topics. Many of the sessions are taught by outsiders.
- We make extensive use of trade shows, seminars, and various association meetings and maintain a log of all external education attendees. Everyone is expected to provide an oral executive summary of the meetings they have attended to their respective mini-company.
- We have a library of books and videos that any associate can borrow. Most of these educational media pertain to training and culture.
- We have internship programs for machining, tool making, EDM, mill right, quality techniques, and mechanical and electrical engineering.
- We encourage our associates to seek and achieve their respective professional certifications, such as the American Society of Quality Control's CQE and CQA certificates and so forth.
- We provide tuition reimbursement for courses in which associates return a documented grade of at least a "C."
- We are very active in working with the schools in our area, as well as with the educational committees of professional associations.

Education is our future. The rate of change mandates that we equip associates with the knowledge needed to compete in the global market. We need to continuously increase our collective intellectual capital.

LIFELONG EDUCATION SCHEDULE

Monday   7:00 a.m., 10:00 a.m., 3:15 p.m.
Tuesday: 6:00 a.m., 3:00 p.m.

title	week of	LLE tape #	instructor(s)
	11/25/96		Thanksgiving week
Storm Water Pollution Prevention	12/2/96	36	Mike
Annual Survey	12/9/96	37	Peter
Dr. John			John Keen
	12/23/96		Christmas Week
	12/30/96		New Years Week
	1/6/97		
QS9000	1/13/97	39	Clark
Sensors and Controls (special schedule)	1/17/97	39	Jeff
Safety	1/20/97	40	Mike & Rose
Plating	1/27/97	41	Mike
Faxing on the Network	2/3/97	42	Linda
	2/10/97		
Ongoing Quality	2/17/97	43	Skills Development Committee
	2/24/97		
Document Manager	3/3/97	44	
QS9000	3/10/97	45	Al
	3/17/97		
P.A.C.T.	3/24/97	46	Rob
SPC9000 Preview/Report	3/31/97	47	Linda
	4/7/97		
8D - Reoccurrence Prevention	4/14/97	48	Al & Mike
	4/21/97		
Safety - First Response Team (special schedule)	4/28/97	49	Mike
	5/5/97		
Gainsharing/Employee Handbook/TRIC	5/12/97	50	Peter
	5/19/97		
#8 Training Grant	5/26/97	51	Fred
	6/2/97		
Herbies & Waste Elimination	6/9/97	52	Rob
Robust Process/PPAP	6/16/97	53	Engineering
	6/23/97		
Dr. John	6/30/97	54	John Keen
8D	7/7/97	55	Mike
	7/14/97		
QS9000 - accessing the manuals "on-line"	7/21/97	56	Al
	7/28/97		
MindShift	8/4/97	57	Peter or Rick
United Way	8/11/97	58	Joe
	8/18/97		
SPC - The Next Level	8/25/97	59	John
	9/1/97		Labor Day

title	week of	LLE tape #	instructor(s)
Training Report	9/8/97	60	
QS9000	9/15/97	56	Al
	9/22/97		
Self-Esteem	9/29/97	57	John Keen
	10/6/97		
	10/13/97		
Vision/Mission	10/20/97	58	Rick & Mike
	10/27/97		
	11/3/97		
	11/17/97		Thanksgiving
QS9000	11/24/97	59	Al
	12/1/97		
	12/8/97		
Annual survey	12/15/97	60	Peter
	12/22/97		Christmas Week
	12/29/98		New Year's Day
	1/5/98		
Quality, QS9000 Update	1/12/98	61	John Timber
	1/19/98		
Culture - Back to Basics	1/26/98	62	John Keen
	2/2/98		
	2/9/98		
Safety	2/16/98	63	Safety Committee
TRIC Revisited, What's New	2/23/98	64	Mike
	3/2/98		
Culture	3/9/98	64	Culture Committee
	3/16/98		
Personality Profile Testing	3/23/98	65	Brad Meyers
Workplace Organization	3/30/98	66	WPO Committee
Tribal History (no 7 a.m. session/Monday)	4/6/98	67	John Keen
	4/13/98		
Problem Solving, Continuous Improvement	4/20/98	68	John
	4/27/98		
	5/4/98		
QS - Are we ready for the Audit?	5/11/98	69	John Timber
Profile Testing cont.	5/18/98	70	Brad Meyers
Tuesday 3 p. m. Make-up (LLE #70)	5/25/98		Memorial Day Week
	6/1/98		
Cost, Wire Show, Germany	6/8/98	71	Peter, Rick, Dick, Dale

MAGIC, INC.

Lifelong Education Class Topic: Habits   Date: 09-29-98

Teacher: JOHN KEEN

This is a summary of the Lifelong Evaluation forms handed out during each class.

1) The trainers were (1-ineffective, 5-effective):

7:00am	10:00am	12:00pm	3:30pm	3:30pm		overall
n/a	n/a	4.67	n/a	n/a		4.67

2) The seminar objectives were (1-confusing, 5-clear):

7:00am	10:00am	12:00pm	3:30pm	3:30pm		overall
n/a	n/a	4.56	n/a	n/a		4.56

3) The overall usefulness of the seminar was(1-not useful, 5-useful):

7:00am	10:00am	12:00pm	3:30pm	3:30pm		overall
n/a	n/a	4.67	n/a	n/a		4.67

4) The pace of the seminar was (1-too fast, 3-just right, 5-too slow):

7:00am	10:00am	12:00pm	3:30pm	3:30pm		overall
n/a	n/a	3.22	n/a	n/a		3.22

Here are some comments from the evaluation forms.

- What did you like best about the seminar?

  ~John's topics always relevant   ~It was fun   ~Helpful hints
  ~Enthusiasm   ~John's motivation   ~The 10% I can remember
  ~Encourage culture of company, and show management respect.

- What did you like least about the seminar?
  ~n/a

- What was the strongest message that you received from this Lifelong Education?

  ~E+R=O   ~Change is good. Take risks.   ~You decide your behavior
  ~Concentrate on the little things. Listen to others.   ~Who I am is important to work on
  ~Identify the good and bad habits, address and alter them.

- What are your recommendations for improvement?

  ~Keep it up John!

- What are your ideas for future topics that would benefit MAGIC?

  ~Steve Covey

TRAINING - SEMINARS - SHOWS - MEETINGS
7/1/98

From	To	What	Where	Who
7/10 7:30am	7/10 5:00pm	Basic operation of screw compressor.	Compressor Tech Inc	Robert Simms
7/10 12:00pm	7/10 1:30 pm	Advanced Manufacturing Academy Board Meetings	Grand Rapids	Mike Langly
7/12 8:24 am	7/12 12 pm	"Designing Sensors in the Tooling - A case Study" by Jeff Lawrence	Cincinnatti, Ohio	Jeff Loginstein
7/16 6:00 pm	7/16 9:00pm	Netware Group Wise, presented by Novell	Pietro's	Linda Williams
7/30 8:00 am	7/30 12:00pm	Wire Mfg Seminar	Muskegon Mi	Dale C, Dave B, Dick C, Tom W.
8/5 8:00 am	8/5 5:00pm	PMA/SMI/NIMS Slideforming standards	Chicago, IL	Mike Langly
8/7 6:00pm	10/16 8pm	Mechanical Inspector Refresher course (Wednesday only)	Grand Rapids, MI	Jennifer Kariden
8/8 1:30pm	8/8 7:00pm	Meridian Industries Supplier Day	Spring Lake, MI	Cindy Woods, Tom Gunderson
8/8 6:00pm	10/10 9:00pm	CQT kRefresher Course - Offered thru Holland ASQ Thursdays, 10weeks	Haworth, Holland, MI	Brian Zimmerman
8/14 12:00pm	8/14 1:30 pm	Advanced Manufacturing Academy Board Meetings	Chicago, IL	Mike Langly
8/19 8:00am	8/19 5:00pm	PMA Technical Sub Committe	Cleveland, OH	Mike Langly
8/20 6:00pm	8/20 9:00pm	Hewlett Packard vs Compaq servers	Grand Rapids, MI	Linda Williams
8/27 8:30am	8/27 4:30pm	PowerPoint 4.0 Advanced Class	Chicago, IL	Christine A, Mary H, Steve L
9/5 12:00pm	9/6 12:00pm	IMTS Show	Chicago, IL	Waun Lynn, Wade Parker
9/5 4:00pm	9/5 9:00pm	Tour of Transmatic and PMA Meeting	Holland, MI	Brian Thurber, Craig Dicson, Dan Dallas, John Timbers, John Langly, Mike Dillion
9/6 8:00am	9/6 5:00pm			

The Magic Workbook, Michigan State University Press, 1999

MAGIC, INC.

138 ERIE ST, CHICAGO IL 60671 • (630) 555-4491 fax (630) 555-0951

April 15, 1998

TO: All MAGIC Associates

FROM: The Culture Committee

The Culture Committee is sponsoring a "JOB SHADOW EXPERIENCE" for associates' children.

The purpose of the "Job Shadow" is to expose students to the potential of different careers available in manufacturing.

The students will be required to write a minimum of a one-page report on what they saw and thought of MAGIC for their school and MAGIC.

We ask that the following guidelines be observed.

> Grades 2nd through 5th - 1/2 day (4 hours)
> Grades 6th through 8th - Full day (6 hours)
> Grades 9th through 12th - Full day (6 hours)

- Notify the office in advance in writing. (Get form from the office.)
- One student in a department at a time. (One per family at a time.)
- Maximum of three students per day. First come, first serve basis.
- No student can run a machine.
- Any day of week. (Except Monday)
- Associate will be responsible for student at all times.
- The student should be exposed to all the departments at MAGIC. This could be done by having a mentor from each department to show the student around.
- The day would start with a General Agenda - reviewing the company history/video- customers - products and safety.

SELECTED READINGS ON WORLD-CLASS OR QUALITY IMPROVEMENTS

BOOK TITLE	AUTHOR
21st CENTURY MANUFACTURING	Thomas G. Gunn
AGENTS OF INFLUENCE	by Pat Choate
AMERICAN SAMURAI, THE	by William Lareau
BUILT TO LAST	James C. Collins & Jerry L. Porr
COACH, THE	by Steven J. Stowell & Matt M. Starcevic
COMPETITIVE ADVANTAGE OF NATIONS	Michael E. Porter
CREATING & ASSURING QUALITY	by Richard Clements
CRISIS & RENEWAL	David K. Hurst
DEMING ROUTE OF QUALITY & PRODUCTIVITY, THE	by William W. Schererbach
DR. DEMING	by Rafael Aquryo
FUTURE OF CAPITALISM, THE	Lester C. Thurow
GOAL, THE	by Eli Goldratt
HEAD TO HEAD	by Lester Thurow
HIGHLY EFFECTIVE PEOPLE	by Stephen R. Covey
HUNTERS AND THE HUNTED, THE	James B. Swartz
IN SEARCH FOR EXCELLENCE	by Tom J. Peter and Robert H. Waterman
JAPAN THAT CAN SAY NO, THE	by Shintaro Ishihara
JAPANESE MANUFACTURING TECHNIQUES	by Richard Schonberger
KAIZEN	by Masaaki Imai
KANBAN - JUST IN TIME AT TOYOTA	Translated by David J. Lu
LEAN THINKING	James P. Womack and Daniel T. Jones
LEARNING ORGANIZATIONS	Sarita Chawla & John Renesch
MACHINE THAT CHANGED THE WORLD M.I.T STUDY, THE	by James Womack
MADE IN AMERICA M.I.T STUDY	Michael L. Dertouzos
MAN WHO DISCOVERED QUALITY, THE	by Andrea Gabor (about Deming)
MANUFACTURING FOR COMPETITIVE ADVANTAGE	by Tom Gunn
NEW MANUFACTURING CHALLENGE, THE	by Kiyoshi Suzaki
NEW SHOP FLOOR MANUFACTURING, THE	Kiyoshi Suzaki
OUT OF THE CRISIS	W. Edwards Deming
SHIGEO SHINGO - SMED SYSTEM	Translated by Andrew P. Dillon
TODAY AND TOMORROW	Henry Ford
WHY AMERICA DOESN'T WORK	by Chuck Colson & Jack Eckerd
WHY THIS HORSE WON'T DRINK	by Ken Matejke
WORLD CLASS MANUFACTURING	by Richard Schonberger
WORLD CLASS MANUFACTURING: THE NEXT DECADE	Richard J. Schoenberger
ZAPP!	by Williams Byhem

CONTINUOUS IMPROVEMENT USER'S GROUP (CIUG)

An additional way to grow people is to make them a part of a continuous improvement users' group (CIUG) in their respective functional area of responsibility. Too many times old paradigms tell us not to share anything with our competitors lest they take advantage of us. This has to change. We are competing in a global market. We can all learn and gain from each other, though if one organization does nothing but soak everything up while giving nothing back, then that company should be invited out of the group.

- Our associates learn from each company they visit. We expect that after each visit we will implement something learned from that company. We have thus become a stronger company because of sharing with others.
- We have sent our associates to Japan, China, Hong Kong, Taiwan, Germany, France, England, and Mexico to check out equipment we are considering purchasing as well as just to benchmark with organizations similar to us. On our associates' recommendation, we have bought equipment that has brought us technology not available in this country. We have received some of these leads to newer technology from our CIUG groups.

- In West Michigan we have a core group of enlightened leaders. Right Place Program sponsors many activities which include the Manufacturesrs Councils and they started the CIUG's in West Michigan. Some of the CIUG groups have been in existence for more than ten years. There are over three hundred companies involved in twenty different functional groups. Examples of some functional groups are: CEOs, Plant Managers, Purchasing, Quality, Human Resources, Sensors and Probes, EDM, Four Slide Setup Reduction, Reengineering, Project Engineers, and Process Engineers.

Another advantage of visiting other places of business is that our people come back appreciating more what we are doing and have accomplished. They appreciate the type of culture that they have at home. In general, we feel that the more exposure we have to practices and technology around the world, the better off we will be. Sharing our own discoveries with other companies is a small price to pay.

We believe in growing our people. They are our most valuable asset and we try to help them grow by exposing them to as many different educational opportunities as possible.

USER GROUPS

ISO/QS-9000

Sensors in Metalforming (SIM)

Concurrent Engineering

Information Technology Management Association (ITMA)

Battenfeld Large Press

Premier Class Injection Molding (PCIM)

Small Manufacturer's User Group III (SMUG)

People Side of Continuous Improvement

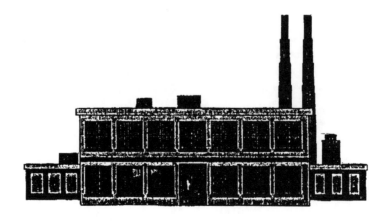

THE KEY TO SURVIVAL

VALUE

☞ Add value without adding cost

☞ Eliminate every cost that doesn't add value

WASTE

THE FOLLOWING EIGHT TYPES OF WASTE WERE FOUND TO BE THE MOST PROMINENT:

1. **Waste from overproduction**

    This is one of the worst wastes, because overproduction covers other problems.

2. **Waste of waiting time**

    This can be due to a lack of parts to work on, watching machines run, etc.

3. **Transportation waste**

    Long transportation distances, double handling, etc. are wastes.

4. **Processing waste**

    This is caused by unnecessary production processes.

5. **Inventory waste**

    Unnecessary inventory covers and/or creates problems.

6. **Waste of motion**

    "Work" is not the same as "move."

7. **Waste from production defects**

    The solution is to make it right the first time!

8. **Not using the talents of all the employees to solve problems.**

PROGRESS FLOW-SKID OF PARTS

	Time	Distance
Receive material/take off truck	10-15 min	80 ft
Inspect & record	20 min	
Put in inventory & record location	15 min	150 ft
Raw material inventory/sit	30 days	
Pull for job order/place in dept	25 min	140 ft
Pick up & set in machine	10 min	20 ft.
Run Part	Seconds	
Store by machine or dept	30 min/24 hrs	
Move to shipping	5 min	150 ft
Prepare outside processing (paint,plate,h/t)	15 min	50 ft
Load truck	10 min	80 ft
Deliver/our truck	45 min?	10 miles
Process/Supplier	(2/3 days) Sec/minute	
Pick-up/our truck	45 min	10 miles
Unload	10 min	80 ft
Inspect	10 min	
Make packaging & weigh skid	15 min	150 ft
Pack	45 min	50 ft
Put in inventory	15 min	75 ft
Ship	345 min, 6 hrs/45 min	1/5 mile, Plus-Storing Plus Trucking

The above charts are used to show associates which steps add value. It, also, shows the time spent at each step and the distance a part would travel in the process.

CIUG PROCESS - ANALYSIS FORM

Directions: Whenever possible, follow an actual task in progress

Write down each step - including "transport, waiting, delay, storage"

Record elapsed time and/or distance traveled

Color in the circle to indicate value-added steps ⟹ ◯

Make some calcuations: (#VA steps/# steps) (VA time/total time)

(distance)

Date: _____   Team/Person: _____

Task Under Investigation: _____

	Step in the Task	Time/Distance
◯		
◯		
◯		
◯		
◯		
◯		
◯		
◯		
◯		
◯		
◯		
◯		

The Magic Workbook, Michigan State University Press, 1999

WHAT ARE JAPANESE/TRANSPLANT CUSTOMERS LOOKING FOR FROM THEIR SUPPLIERS?

KAIZEN

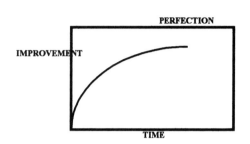

KAIZEN

DELIVERY KAIZEN

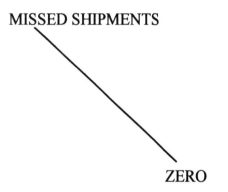

MISSED SHIPMENTS

ZERO

TECHNICAL SPEED OF RESPONSE
KAIZEN

(DESIGN/QUOTATION/TOOLING/PROTOTYPES/SAMPLES)

SHORTER LEAD TIMES

COST KAIZEN

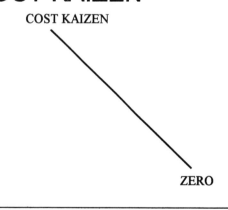

COST KAIZEN

ZERO

PROFIT	PRICE LESS COST
NOT	
PRICE	COST PLUS PROFIT

QUALITY KAIZEN

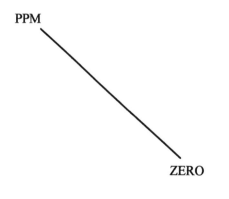

PPM

ZERO

HIGHER QUALITY LEADS TO LOWER COST

REQUIREMENTS FOR
"WORLD CLASS"

1. LESS THAN 0 PPM REJECTS

2. 100% ON-TIME DELIVERY

3. 50% OR BETTER VALUE ADDED - INVENTORY - MACHINERY - PAYROLL

4. LESS THAN 2% COST OF QUALITY - QA

   DEPARTMENT/TRAINING/ SCRAP/RETURNS/REWORK

5. EMPLOYEE INVOLVEMENT (OWNERSHIP)

"KAIZEN"
TOOL

CONTINUOUS IMPROVEMENT

MEANS

TRAINING AND EDUCATION

The Magic Workbook, Michigan State University Press, 1999

KEY PERFORMANCE INDICATORS (MAGIC REPORT CARD)

| | QUALITY | | | | | PROFIT | COST | | | DELIVERY | SAFETY | MORALE |
	PPM	C of Q	CPK	RETURNS & ALLOWANCES	CUSTOMER CONCERNS		SALES	SALES/PAYROLL INCREASE	INVENTORY AS % OF SALES DECREASE			
GOAL	<70/MILLION	<2.0% MO.	>1.75 MO.	<$ .3% MO.	10 / MO.	>6% PRE TAX						
JANUARY												
FEBRUARY												
MARCH												
APRIL												
MAY												
JUNE												
JULY												
AUGUST												
SEPTEMBER												
OCTOBER												
NOVEMBER												
DECEMBER												

ID	Task Name	DUR	RES	S	F	Gantt chart
1	Quality KPI	306d		9/1	11/1	
2	Gage for D-5611	15d	JG	10/7	10/27	100%
3	Gage for D-53344	50d	JG	10/24	1/1	100%
4	Gage for R-2172	42d	JG,JT	1/1	2/27	95%
5	Gage for 332425	60d		2/1	4/24	Require gage instructions
6	Gage for SR6827	60d		12/1	2/22	10% offering to help build gage / 95% Require gage instructions
7	Gage for SR6254	90d		5/1	9/3	
8	Gage for SR6542	90d		6/3	10/4	
9	Gage for 5214	90d		7/1	11/1	
10	Gage for 5514	90d		3/1	7/4	
11	Gage for 10585	90d		5/1	9/3	
12	Gage for 13744/45	90d		6/3	10/4	
13	Gage for 6081	30d		3/1	4/11	
14	Gage for 1400	90d		4/1	8/2	
15	Gage for 3340	90d		4/1	8/2	
16	Gage for 79652	90d		5/1	9/3	
17	Conveyor for Press #6	56d	DW,S	10/16	1/1	100%

Page 1

ID	Task Name	DUR	RES	S	F						
18	Straightener for Press #8	75d	DW,JI	10/2	1/12	70%					
19	Tool Maintenance Kit	76d	WP	9/1	12/15	Task on hold					
20	Cost KPI	76d		9/1	12/15	% ating responsibility to toolmakers					
21	Cost of Quality sheet	21d	JT,JG	9/1	10/1	% a informal system					
22	Parts counter	55d	DW,JI	10/1	12/15	25% ond parts counter on order					
23	H.T. oven for toolroom.	55d	WP	10/1	12/15	15% Wade has information.					
24	Delivery KPI	90d		11/1	3/5						
25	Percent on-time delivery	90d		11/1	3/5	97%					
26	Safety KPI	114d		10/2	3/7						
27	OSHA guards all presses	60d	Maint.	12/15	3/7	40% s for Presses 4,6,7 complete; 1 in-prog; 2 on order					
28	WPO (Win once a qtr.)	28d	PR	10/2	11/8	0%					
29	Scrap belt for press #5	53d	JD	10/2	12/13	100%					
30	Moral KPI	0d		12/1	12/1						
31	Mountain Jacks outing	0d		12/1	12/1	Planning outing for Feb.					

Page 2

A Gantt chart for press guard installation projects.

ID	Task Name	DUR	S	F	Timeline notes
1	**Press #1**	0d	1/22	1/22	
2	Improve interlocks	30d	1/29	3/8	0% — New system in house
3	Partition front guard	30d	1/29	3/8	50%
4	Counterbalance front guard	30d	1/29	3/8	0%
5	Build, partition, and install part out guard	30d	1/29	3/8	50% — Design complete, began building frame
6	Build and install feeder side guard	30d	1/29	3/8	50% — Design complete, began building frame
7	Interlock feeder pin	30d	1/29	3/8	0%
8	Add interlock to rear guard	30d	1/29	3/8	0%
9	**Press #2**	0d	1/22	1/22	
10	Install a new interlock system	40d	1/22	3/15	0% — New guard ordered, due by 3/1
11	Build and install feeder guard	25d	1/22	2/23	100% — New guard ordered, due by 3/1
12	Build and install front/part out guard	40d	1/22	3/15	0% — New guard ordered, due by 3/1
13	Build and install rear guard	25d	1/22	2/23	100% — New guard ordered, due by 3/1
14	Build and install slider system	40d	1/22	3/15	0% — New guard ordered, due by 3/1
15	Build and install guard counter balance	40d	1/22	3/15	0% — New guard ordered, due by 3/1
16	**Press #3**	0d	1/22	1/22	
17	Install a new interlock system	45d	1/22	3/22	0% — Depends upon outcome of press #2
18	Build and install feeder guard	45d	1/22	3/22	100% — Depends upon outcome of press #2
19	Build and install front/part out guard	45d	1/22	3/22	0% — Depends upon outcome of press #2
20	Build and install rear guard	45d	1/22	3/22	100% — Depends upon outcome of press #2
21	Build and install slider system	45d	1/22	3/22	0% — Depends upon outcome of press #2
22	Build and install guard counter balance	45d	1/22	3/22	0% — Depends upon outcome of press #2
23	**Press #4**	0d	1/22	1/22	
24	Improve interlocks	10d	1/22	2/2	100%
25	Heighten front guard 10" (control side)	10d	1/22	2/2	100%
26	Partition front guard 4"	10d	1/22	2/2	100%
27	Trim part out guard	10d	1/22	2/2	100%
28	Lower back guard 6"	10d	1/22	2/2	100%
29	Partition back guard 4"	10d	1/22	2/2	100%

Page 1

The Magic Workbook, Michigan State University Press, 1999

ID	Task Name	DUR	S	F	Timeline / % / Notes
30	Counter balnce front and rear guards	10d	1/22	2/2	100%
31	Press #5	0d	1/22	1/22	◆
32	Improve interlocks	40d	1/22	3/15	0%
33	Partition part out guard	40d	1/22	3/15	50%
34	Pin or interlock feeder guards	40d	1/22	3/15	0%
35	Repair rear guard	40d	1/22	3/15	100%
36	Lock part out guard with front guard	40d	1/22	3/15	0%
37	Press #6	0d	1/22	1/22	◆
38	Install a new interlock system	10d	1/22	2/2	100% — Install interlock on front feeder guard
39	Build and intall front/partout guard	10d	1/22	2/2	100%
40	Build and install slider system	10d	1/22	2/2	100%
41	Build and install guard counter balance	10d	1/22	2/2	100%
42	Build and install feeder guards	50d	1/22	3/29	0% — Waiting on new feeder
43	Install rear guard	1d	1/22	1/22	100%
44	Press #7	0d	1/22	1/22	◆
45	Improve interlock system	40d	1/22	3/15	100% — completed on 2/23/96
46	Build, partition and install feeder guard	40d	1/22	3/15	100% — completed on 2/23/96
47	Build, partition and install part out guard	40d	1/22	3/15	100% — completed on 2/23/96
48	Interlock rear door guard	40d	1/22	3/15	100% — completed on 2/23/96
49	Build and intall a new front guard	40d	1/22	3/15	100% — completed on 2/23/96
50	Press #8	0d	1/22	1/22	◆
51	Improve interlock system	35d	1/22	3/8	0% — Depends upon outcome of press #2
52	Build and install a new feeder guard	35d	1/22	3/8	100% — Depends upon outcome of press #2
53	Build and install a new front/partout guard	35d	1/22	3/8	0% — Depends upon outcome of press #2
54	Roller system	35d	1/22	3/8	0% — Depends upon outcome of press #2
55	Build and install counter balance	35d	1/22	3/8	0% — Depends upon outcome of press #2
56	Build and intall rear guard	35d	1/22	3/8	100% — Depends upon outcome of press #2
57	Guard the transfer	35d	1/22	3/8	0% — Depends upon outcome of press #2
58					

Timeline header: January — 14, 21, 28; February — 4, 11, 18, 25; March — 3, 10, 17, 24, 31; April — 7, 14, 21

Page 2

MINI-COMPANY

We have been using the mini-company concept for several years, following Kiyoshi Suzaki's book *The New Shop Floor Management*. The basic idea is that everyone working for the company is the president of his or her respective responsibility. Achieving buy-in to this concept is difficult. Each department is considered a mini-company. Everyone in the company as a whole is assigned to one mini-company. Each mini-company usually has three officers to run weekly meetings and make monthly reports to the internal bankers (the president, general manager, plant manager, and engineering manager).

Each mini-company has a specific resource person assigned to it from the technical and quality departments to facilitate communications and decisions. At weekly meetings, the resource individuals appear for the first part of the meeting so that they can be informed, provide feedback, or help with discussions pertaining to their respective areas of expertise.

- The major driving force behind the mini-company is the measurement system of Quality, Cost, Delivery, Safety, and Morale (QCDS& M). Each mini-company is required in coordination with the corporate measurements to develop their own measurements of QCDS&M. Before the start of a new year, at the internal bankers' meeting, goals for each measurement are proposed and accepted by the bankers.

- Monthly results are posted and referred to as Key Performance Indicators [KPI]. Some organizations refer to these as "Dashboards." The mini-company KPI boards are kept in each company's area and reviewed at weekly meetings. Each month a permanent score is recorded on the board in either green, red, or blue. Green means that the mini-company has exceeded the goal for this period, red means the goal has not been achieved, and blue means the goal has not been met but has been improved upon over the prior month. Color coding and the visual board are very effective.

- Somewhere in each mini-company is a standardized problem-solving board referred to as the "Continuous Improvement Story." The problem being solved comes directly from the red column on the KPI board.

Reports have improved from simple charts to multicolored graphs to Power Point presentations. Real-world bankers would delight in seeing these reports from the people who make things happen on the factory floor.

- Once a year all the mini-company officers observe the other companies' presentations to learn new ideas and improve their own reports. All the reports are available for anyone to review.

- Twice a year we shut down the plant to have a trade show. Everyone brings a dish to share for lunch. Each mini-company shows and tells what they have accomplished in the past six months. Everyone has a chance to see each mini-company's presentation.

SPRING MINI-CO QUARTERLY BANKERS REPORT

3rd quarter fiscal 1998   *Jan 98 - Mar 98*

Officers: Dale Cooper   Mathew Worden
              Dick Campeau   Fern Quintellia

Spring Torsion 3rd Quarter 1998 Analysis

What went right:
- Internal scrap reduction.

- Noticable process improvements (reduce double handling)
- Cross training & skill improvement
- Maintaining very low PPM.
- Machine #1 & #2 thru one oven.

What went wrong:
- 2nd shift operator position.

What was learned:
- Over & over trng and reminders required. Can't get lazy or you slip into old habits. Some old fixes are paying off. (V78250 & 17604 / 05)
- In-Line ovens working great !! Machine #1 & #2. Calsonic Kan Ban.
- Set-ups willing to do more tooling. Keep challenging them !
- Our system working well. Tough part is how to get to the next level ?
- Get set-ups input. Gives em ownership.

What was learned:
- Either we are not clear enough up front with the requirements or we may want to look for someone with different strengths

ISSUES:
- **Personnel.** 2nd shift operator. Do we limit ourselves to pre-set people as operators?
- **Torque testing.** Frame built & components mounted. Must keep the process team focused.
- **Reel storage.** Must work with Brad on reducing storage quantity with Spekker. (Currently 50)
- **Full time Quality Resource.** Long-term something to keep in mind.
- **Lack of gauges put to floor.** Considering other options. [Could each set-up be responsible for their own gauges?]
- **Smoking table.** We can smell it in the spring area. Need some sort of ventilation near the table.

	1st Quarter	2nd Quarter	3rd Quarter	Change	Comments
Tor Scrap	179,000 parts	163,106 parts	91,426	**44%** ⇩	
Comp Scrap	22,497 parts	140,163 parts	31,950	**77%** ⇩	
All Scrap	201,497	303,269	123,376	**60%** ⇩	
$ Scrap	$7,061	$7,541	$3,407	**55%** ⇩	
$ Rework	$803.00	$828.00	$372	**56%** ⇩	
$ Sales	$526,000	$582,000	$634,000	**9%** ⇧	
Sales / Payroll	$6.03 avg	$6.49 avg	$6.75	**4%** ⇧	
Inventory	14.83 days (avg)	15.33 days (avg)	15.66 days (avg)	*1%* ⇧	
Delivery	99% avg	98.7% avg	99.4% avg	*.8%* ⇧	
WCI's	65	61.5	64	**4%** ⇧	
Attendance	28 occurrences	22 occurrences	14	**36%** ⇩	

Bold: Meeting goals or positive trends
Italic: Not meeting goals or negative trends

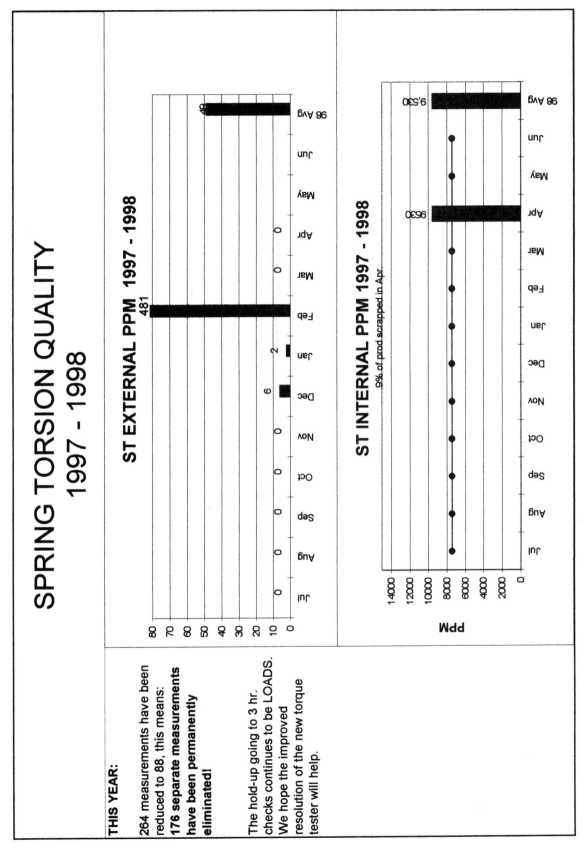

SPRING TORSION QUALITY
1997 - 1998

ST EXTERNAL PPM 1997 - 1998

ST INTERNAL PPM 1997 - 1998
9% of prod scrapped in Apr.

THIS YEAR:

264 measurements have been reduced to 88, this means: **176 separate measurements have been permanently eliminated!**

The hold-up going to 3 hr. checks continues to be LOADS. We hope the improved resolution of the new torque tester will help.

SPRING TORSION QUALITY
1997 - 1998

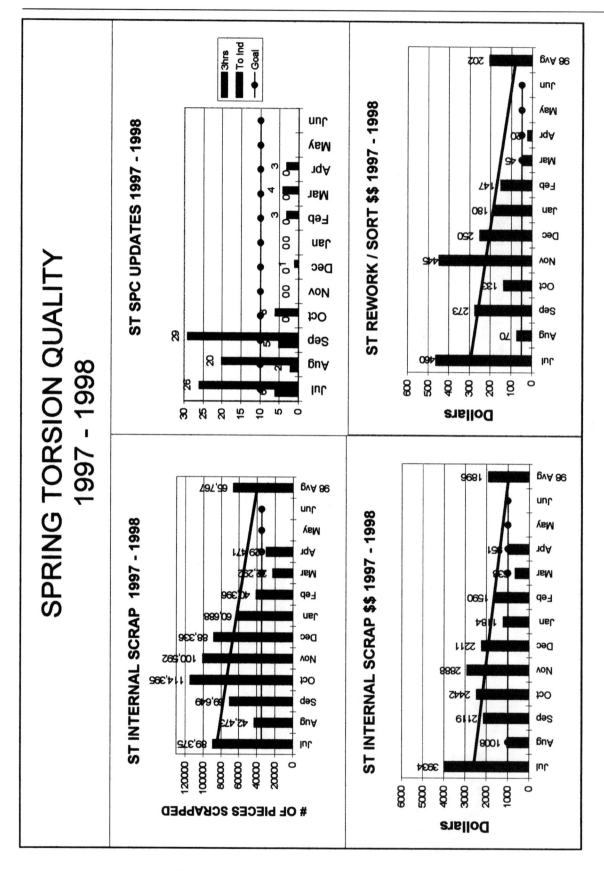

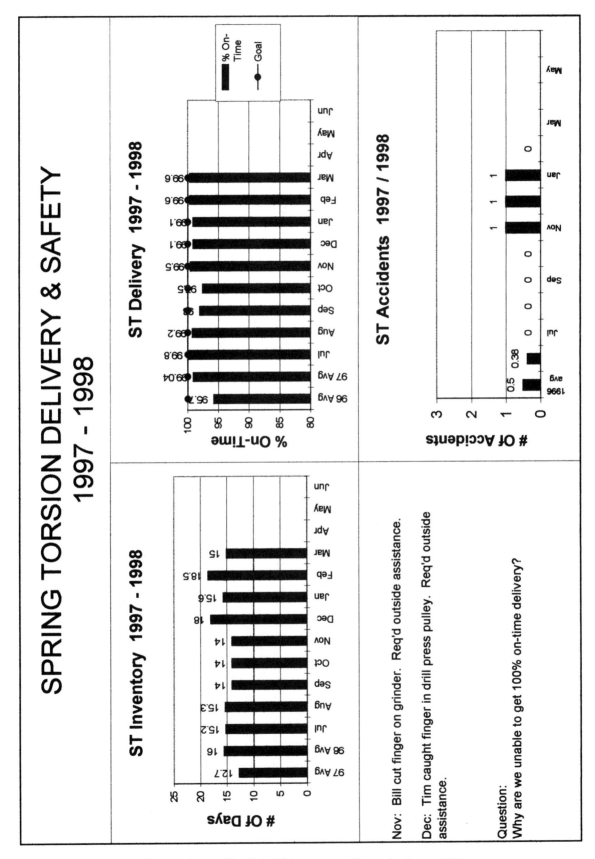

SPRING TORSION DELIVERY & SAFETY
1997 - 1998

ST Delivery 1997 - 1998

% On-Time

96 Avg	95.7
97 Avg	99.04
Jul	99.8
Aug	99.2
Sep	99
Oct	99.5
Nov	99.5
Dec	99.1
Jan	99.1
Feb	99.6
Mar	99.6

Legend: % On-Time, Goal

ST Accidents 1997 / 1998

Of Accidents

1996 avg: 0.5, 0.38
Jul: 0
Sep: 0
Nov: 1, 1
Jan: 1, 0

ST Inventory 1997 - 1998

Of Days

97 Avg	12.7
98 Avg	16
Jul	15.2
Aug	15.3
Sep	14
Oct	14
Nov	14
Dec	18
Jan	15.6
Feb	18.5
Mar	15

Nov: Bill cut finger on grinder. Req'd outside assistance.

Dec: Tim caught finger in drill press pulley. Req'd outside assistance.

Question:
Why are we unable to get 100% on-time delivery?

SPRING TORSION MORALE
1997 - 1998

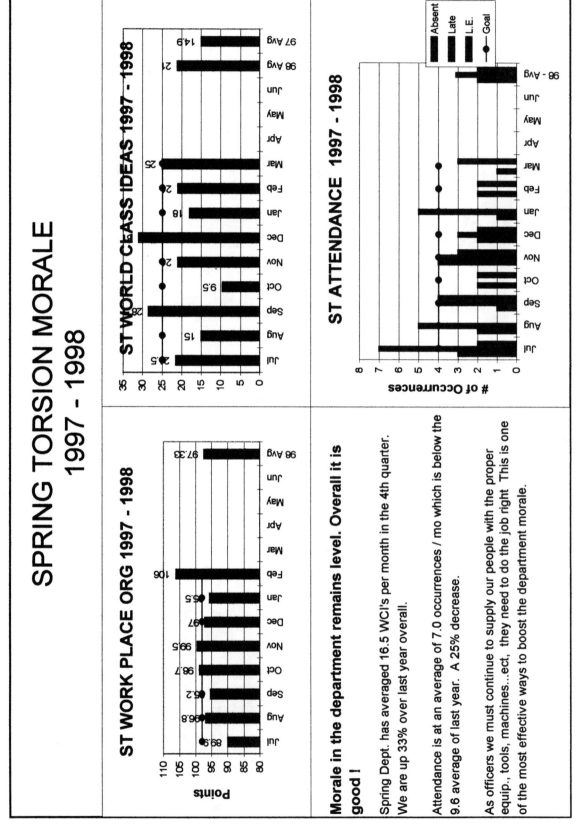

ST WORLD CLASS IDEAS 1997 - 1998

	Jul	Aug	Sep	Oct	Nov	Dec	Jan	Feb	Mar	Apr	May	Jun	98 Avg	97 Avg
	25.5	15	28	9.5	21		18	21	25				21	14.9

ST ATTENDANCE 1997 - 1998

Legend: Absent, Late, L.E., Goal

# of Occurrences

| | Jul | Aug | Sep | Oct | Nov | Dec | Jan | Feb | Mar | Apr | May | Jun | 98 - Avg |

ST WORK PLACE ORG 1997 - 1998

Points

	Jul	Aug	Sep	Oct	Nov	Dec	Jan	Feb	Mar	Apr	May	Jun	98 Avg
	89.9	96.8	96.2	98.7	99.5	97	96.5	106					97.33

Morale in the department remains level. Overall it is good !

Spring Dept. has averaged 16.5 WCI's per month in the 4th quarter. We are up 33% over last year overall.

Attendance is at an average of 7.0 occurrences / mo which is below the 9.6 average of last year. A 25% decrease.

As officers we must continue to supply our people with the proper equip., tools, machines...ect, they need to do the job right This is one of the most effective ways to boost the department morale.

98

TASK ASSIGMENT LOG - SPRING TORSION MINI COMPANY

DT	Team	Assignment	Target Date	Status	%	Comments
		Reviewed on 7/13/98				
3/19/98	DD/KV	Barnley & Boulder directly into tubs	10/1/98	Design	25	Basic Idea / ordering materials
3/19/98	MS/DC	Crest's plans for certified supplier (30 prints)	5/1/00	In-Work	25	Implementing plan of action. (1 prt / month)
3/19/98	DD/DC/MS	Develope ST training / Complete tsk log	11/15/98	In-Work	65	Torque tests / training is next hurdle
3/19/98	GZ/KV	Implement New Torque Tester	8/15/98	In-Work	95	Next, begin testing on 1st part
3/19/98	KV	MCT oil wheels	10/1/98	Design	10	Considering options
3/24/98	KV	Oil catch tray for Mings				Priority?
3/24/98	KV / JL	Laser sensor on a Ming		Design		Priority?
3/24/98	KV	Oiler on Steelcase 4200				Priority?
3/24/98	KV	Chute for 17604 / 05		Design done	25	Priority?
3/24/98	KV / set-ups	Dowel Pins for Ming #9 & 10				Priority?
3/24/98	KV	Sensors on Mings (& the air lines)			25	Priority? Parts on-hand
3/2/98	KV	Gauge. VB3958		Design done		Priority? Ready to build.
3/2/98	KV	Guage. 16876 / 16877		Design done		Priority? Ready to build.
3/2/98	KV	Guage. 39160		Design done		Priority? Ready to build.
3/2/98	KV	Guage. A92000198-00		Design done		Priority? Ready to build.
3/2/98	KV	Guage. 87830 / 87831		Design done		Priority? Ready to build.

(right margin vertical label: GAUGES)

PR Bankers Report

2nd Quarter '98

Thursday, January 29, 1998

Table of Contents:

Business Plan Update:

Standard Work
1. ECR/PCR forms
   * Still working well, we started segregating the sheets that have been turned in for "out of spec." dimensions

2. Work Instructions
   * Incorporating these into our Training program. Working on completing "finishing a job" and "starting a job"

Tooling (Robust, on time, Preventative Maintenance
1. Process improvements
   * R-3026 (Grid stamping) is die of the month
   * 30463 up next.
2. Tool maintenance program.
   * Working on structure of it now.
3. Preventative Maintenance
   * A lubricant company is coming in on 1/28/98. Will share their proposal on new PM Sheets.

Material
1. Box changers
   * Started utilizing our large box changer more effectively. We are limited due to the size of the box changer.
   * Proposed 3 new box changers – (see corporate concerns)
2. Scrap Removal.
   * Status: New dies are being looked at for scrap removal. We have incorporated changes to the dies to help reduce scrap and parts coming off in the same area.

Equipment
1. 1 gage built each month
   * 1 Gage built to check the 1502/006 1502/005 and 502/150 502/151 502/152 lock bars
   * Boulder Corp. fixture is built.
3. Centralized Equipment
   * Moved our SPC stations to a more centrally located area.
   * Material racks have been put in place and look great.
   * Die racks moved to help alleviate space

2nd Quarter Summary

- 160 World Class Ideas (139.3 points) for the Quarter
- New computer stations added.
- Adjustable air lines on presses
- Painting of die racks, gage cabinets...etc
- 502-006/007 die.
- Start of 3rd shift.
- Lubrication issues – good progress with the lubricant company
- Feeder for Press #3
- Adding Bliss to help production requirements.
- Training Meeting – Start of production procedures book.
- ECR/PCR'S started.
- Customer Visits – more to come
- Internal Audit Sheet completed, will start doing again as of 2/2/98 (2x monthly)

Corporate Concerns :

1. **Box Changers**
   Would like the o.k. to purchase 3 more box changers
   1 – similar to the one on Press #9, (24" ∅ in size) Quoted $3,995/ea.
   2 - larger in size for presses 2/3/5/8 (32" ∅ in size) Quoted $4,995/ea.

   We started utilizing a box changer on the R-3026 (Brass Grid Stamping). We gathered some information on how many parts we produce on average per shift. Below are the results.

   Without box changer
   - 10 separate runs (20 shifts) Average = 13,275 parts per shift.

   With box changer
   - 3 shifts using box changer Average 19,833 parts per shift.
   - Average of 6,560 more parts produced per shift.

   ❑ In addition to the above info, the box changer built internally has considerably helped with our back log on presses 6 and 9. The high volume jobs like the Donnelly 10585 and Prince V-79552 are no longer consistently past due. The box changers allow for uninterupted running.

2. **Conveyors** - A constraint has developed in the last few weeks with additional conveyors required to run the channel, 502-006 / 007 and the Bliss press requires conveyors for scrap and parts.
   - Would like the o.k. to purchase 2 new conveyors (getting quoted!)
     - ❑ 1 @ 14" long (10" wide)
     - ❑ 1 @ 20" long (14" wide)

3. **Lubricant Issues** – Still working with the lubricant company.

4. **Process Improvement List** – we have several little items on the list along with some bigger items.

5. **Caseys (32278 lens closeout)** – Who has the ball in terms of PVC coated stainless. We 100% audited last shipment for dirty parts and still had parts returned. We will continue at solving this problem

6. **Connley Packaging Issues** – Connley has attempted to return parts based on our quoted packaging method. Cost issue?? What level of involvement should the Press Room take?

7. **Heavy duty bander** – to be used on heavier material.

8. **#4 Feeder** - Mechanical to Servo feed. Been having several problems as of late and with the addition of the world detachment clip. We should look at this carefully.

9. **Coffee Pot** – o.k. to move one closer to Press Room. Current coffee pot is too far away. A coffee area located between VA, PR , PR Tooling and Maintenance would be ideal.

Tooling Improvements:

- Red tag dies at an all time low (one week at red tag dies)
- inge running (7 weeks without running old die)
- 52344 Stud die running consistently.
- Rebuilt 502-006 and 502-009
- Channel ECN adding holes.
- Rebuilt HAY022 clevis die.
- Rebuilt AB and BA.
- GE-213719-2
- Rebuilt V-67895
- 10585 rebuilt
- 107671 – rebuilding die. ½ complete….due 2/4/98
- Re-built 67011/010 blank die.

1st Quarter vs. 2nd Quarter KPI'S

	1998 - 1st Qtr.	1998 - 2nd Qtr.	Difference
PPM (total)	30,099	4,379	**-25,720**
Concerns (total)	11.0	19.0	**+8**
Sales (total)	$ 2,512,000	$2,740,000	**+ $228,000**
Sales to Payroll (ave/month)	$7.66	$8.93	**+ $1.30**
Delivery (ave/month)	95.9%	95.6%	**- 0.33%**
Total Accidents	6	4	**- 2.0**
Inventory (ave/month)	5.2	5.8	**+ 0.6**
WPO Score (monthly ave.)	88.8%	92.3%	**+ 3.0%**
Attendance	26.0	14.0	**- 12.0**
WCI'S (total)	79.83	136.4	**+ 56.57 ideas**
Press Up-Time (ave/month)	28.3	29.9	**+ 1.6 hours**

Quality

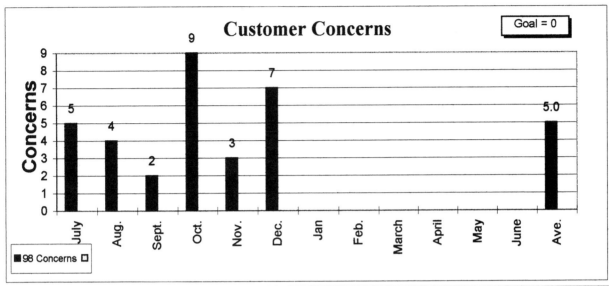

Customer Concerns Goal = 0

Parts Per Million Goal = 0

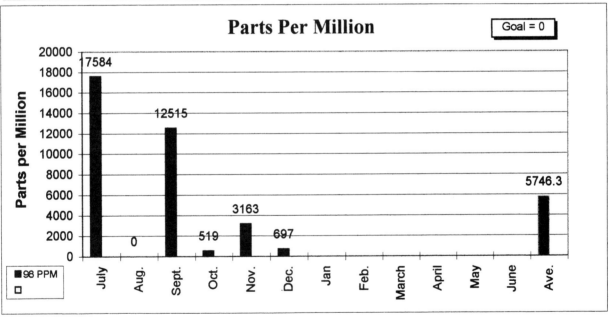

KPI'S FOR PRESS ROOM

Cost

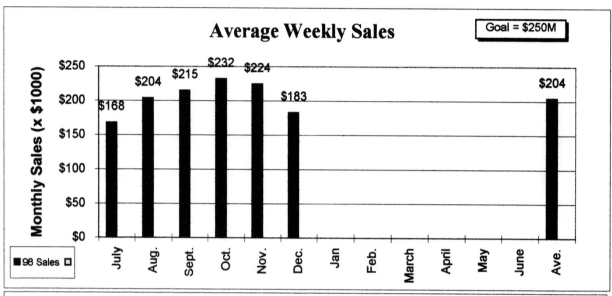

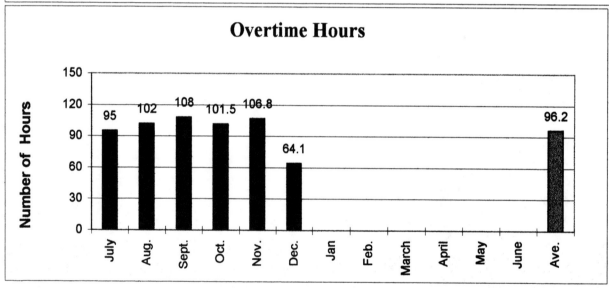

Cost

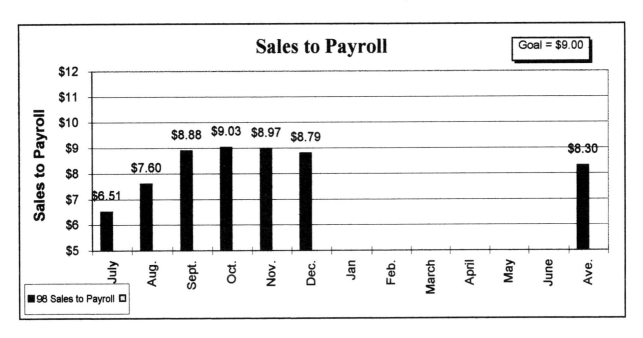

Delivery

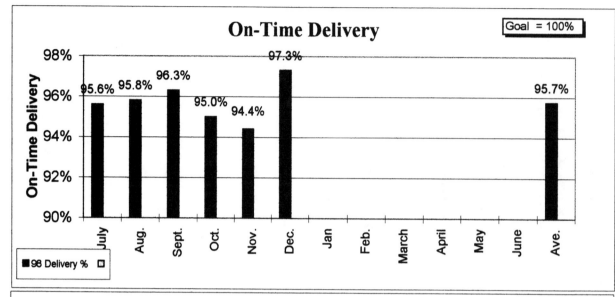

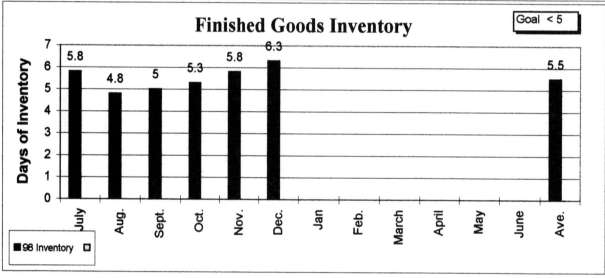

The Magic Workbook, Michigan State University Press, 1999

Safety

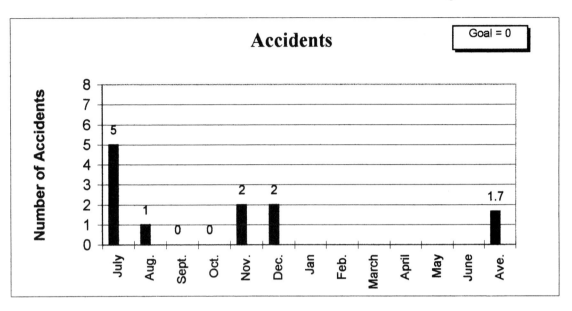

Morale

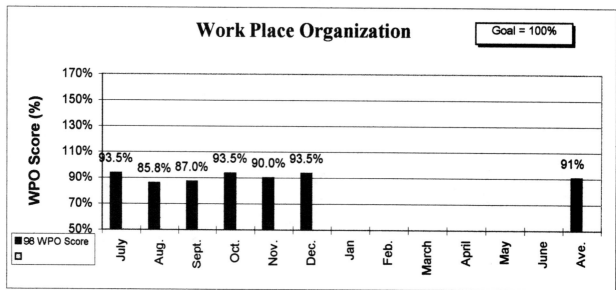

Work Place Organization

Goal = 100%

WPO Score (%)

170%
150%
130%
110%
90%
70%
50%

93.5% 85.8% 87.0% 93.5% 90.0% 93.5%   91%

■ 98 WPO Score
□

July Aug. Sept. Oct. Nov. Dec. Jan Feb. March April May June Ave.

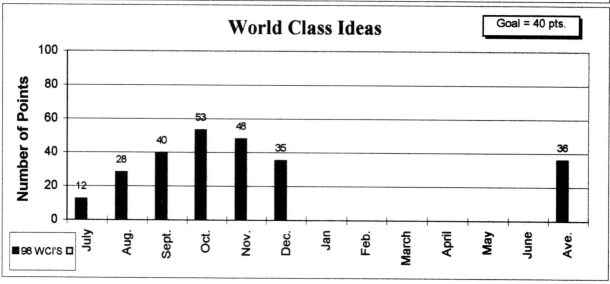

World Class Ideas

Goal = 40 pts.

Number of Points

100
80
60
40
20
0

12 28 40 53 48 35   36

■ 98 WCI'S □

July Aug. Sept. Oct. Nov. Dec. Jan Feb. March April May June Ave.

Morale

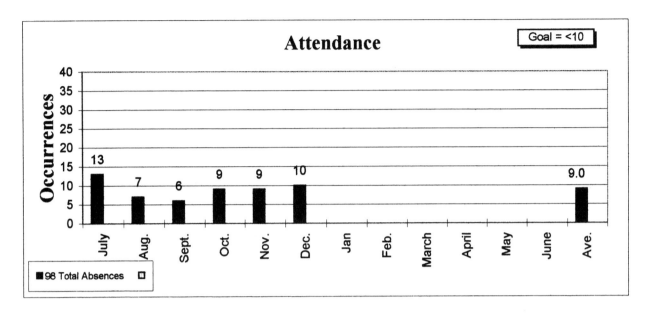

FOUR SLIDE MINI- COMPANY
AUGUST 1998 BANKERS REPORT
PRESENTED ON : SEPT. 24, 1998

TABLE OF CONTENTS

FS Quality Fiscal 1999

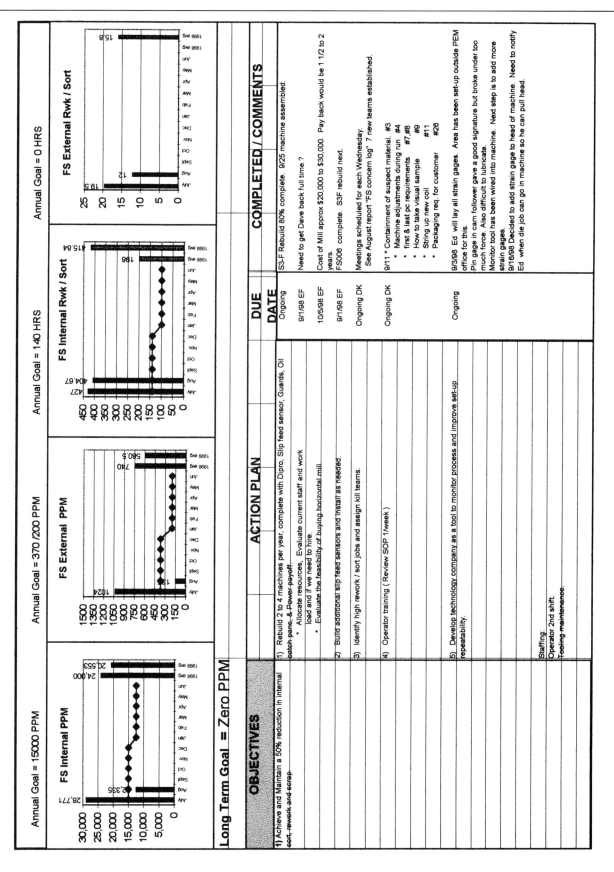

Current 8D Teams

Customer	Part Number	Team	Problem	Internal?	External?	Status	
Applegate	GRRT4858131087	Dan, Rick Tom (leader)	Large Whisker of Excess Material on tab	X		Update from Tom ,John 9/23	Last run - part has slug marks, burr
Scotch	2471-6401	Ed , Ed , Dick Dan (leader)	Gap too large, barbs misformed, radius on leg bad	X		Re-Assigned Kill Team 9/23	
Boulder	All reflectors	Dan, Ed, Alan Jeff (leader)	Oil	X		Update from Jeff - 9/23	
Advantage	GRRT4858131090	Jack, Joe Tom (leader)	Missing Relief Notch Misformation		X	Meeting 9/23/98 8:00 AM	
Boulder	30275	Chris, John Joe (leader)	Wings, Slug marks	X		Update from John 9/23	Currently sorting for this condition
Boulder	16739	Alan, Ed, Dan Jim (leader)	Misformed part		X	Need pull test from Boulder	Pull test finish 2 weeks-deviation extended until 10/24/98
Boulder	30072	Josh, Dan Ed (leader)	Bent		X	Light curtain sensor update	Ed F - 9/23/98
Boulder	30598	Alan, Jims, Mike, Joe (leader)	Barbs too small		X	Meeting 9/23/98 3:00 PM	
Boulder	30655 / 30656	Ed, Tim Jack (leader)	Scratches, Misfeeds	X		on sensor list Ed -9/23	
Badger	All jobs with coolant,etc.	Ed , Tim, Alan Jeff (leader)	Coolant is not always turned on when should be	X		Meeting 9/23/98 7:00 AM	
Capitol	17766-SOX-A010	Ed, John Tim (leader)	Misfeed	X		on sensor list Ed 9/23/98	
M.C.	4168122	Josh, Scott, Dennis (leader)	Legs uneven	X		Update from Scott 9/23	Possible sensors
Badger	6400	Jim, Mike Mike (leader)	Misfeed	X		Temp fix Mike 9/23	setup for sensors
Boulder	12928	Chris, John Scott (leader)	Misformed part		X	Possible sensor Ed - 9/23	
Boulder	85199	Josh, Ed Rick (leader)	Misformed part		X	Bihler Run October 5	

Leaders: Make sure you note your highlighted section for meeting time and make sure all team members are present in F/S office at that time.
If highlighted section shows "Update" Deb will just need information from assigned person only.

14 TEAMS OPEN CONCERNS
4 CLOSED CONCERNS

August FourSlide Concern Log

CUSTOMER	PART NUMBER	MACHINE NUMBER	SET-UP	ASSIGNED OPERATOR	DISCOVER BY	DATE	INT	EXT	DEFECT	QUANTITY SCRAPPED	REASON (IF KNOWN)	ACTION PLAN
Badger	246781-4910	4	Tim	Mark	Jim	8/3/98	X		Part is Cocked / not flat	2265		Jim assigned to Corrective Action
AGS Hills	70400-30125	9	Dennis	Josh	Mark	8/4/98	X		Misformed	1320		Working on new tool
AGS Hills	70400-30125	9	Dennis	Josh	Mark	8/4/98	X		Flatness out of spec	3197		Working on new tool
Kingman	7713C52H01	6	Chris C	Mark	Mark	8/5/98	X		Burrs	1633		
Boulder	30576	2	Joe B	Josh	Josh	scrap from 6/30	X		Scratches	4264		Corrected - verification runs (5)
Advantage	GRRT4858131090	19	Jack	Mike	Mike	8/6/98	X		Misformed	1235	Pin Broke	Assigned - see "Current 8d Teams"
Advantage	GRRT4858131090	19	Jack	Mike	Joel	8/7/98	X		Misformed	2	Pin Broke	
Boulder	32234	2	Dan K	Mark	Mark	8/6/98	X		Misfeed	1008		
AGS Hills	31636	15	Joe	Josh	A	8/10/98	X		Too long, too short	70		8d complete - sent on to Logansport
Seat City	600126	3	Dan	Mark	Mark	8/10/98	X		Misformed	20	Material Wrapped around swift	
Applegate	GRRT4858131087	13	Jack	Josh	Josh	8/10/98	X		Burrs, Feed, Misform	4486		Assigned - see "Current 8d Teams"
Boulder	30276	5	Jim	Mark	Mark	8/10/98	X		Bump Height Out - high	1752		
Seat City	600126	3	Dan	Mark	Mark	8/10/98	X		Slug Marks	765		
Terra Valley	150818	12	Roger	Josh	Tim	8/11/98	X		Misform, Out of spec Parts cockeyed	7000	Front tool needed rocklinized forgot to set	Added reminder to set-up sheet
Boulder	32371	14	Chris	Josh	Eng Sample	8/13/98		X	Overall Height out low	3432	No first piece done	Mini-Co meeting - Reminder 1st pc
Terra Valley	151325	13	Roger	Josh	Josh	8/13/98	X		Misformed	200		
Badger	AA116572-0570	9	Jim	Mark	Mark	8/14/98	X		Foot Height out of spec	1566		
Boulder	30072	3	Chris	Mark	Mark	8/17/98	X		Slots uneven	3035		Assigned - see "Current 8d Teams"
Atlas	000-0163	10	Dennis	Josh	Dennis	8/18/98	X		Burr	802	Cutter Broke	Corrected - verification runs (5)
Atlas	000-0163	10	Dennis	Josh	Josh	8/18/98	X		Length too long, Burrs	2354	Cutter Broke	Established tolerance at customer
Waters	32026	5	Chris	Joel	Mark	8/19/98	X		Wings	12483		
Boulder	30072	3	Chris	Mark	A	8/20/98	X		Misformed	65		
Waters	32026	5	Chris	Joel	Josh	8/20/98	X		Height to lance too low	2269		
Badger	AA146522-6971	No Traceability	Tim	Mike	Jim	8/21/98	X		90 deg angle out (93.06)	4570	No coolant turned on parts	Assigned - see "Current 8d Teams"
Millbrook	17515	13	Tim	Mike	Tim	8/19/98	X		Blue ink on parts	1701	on interior of coil	Brad given samples, info
Boulder	12928	4	Jim	Mark	C	8/25/98		X	Misform	29	Post Broke	Assigned - see "Current 8d Teams"
Boulder	85199	11	Mike	Mike	C	8/25/98		X	Misform	111	Wire diving	Assigned - see "Current 8d Teams"
Boulder	30275	1	Dan	Mark	Mike	8/26/98	X		Angle out of spec high	3778		
Scotch	2471-6001	13	Chris	Mark	Mark	8/27/98	X		Slug marks distort prts	2937		
Kingman	7713C50H02	13	Roger	Josh	Eng Sample	8/26/98		X	New design did not work	2672	Meeting with Kingman Group	Working on design change
Oak	MS1-75035-02	11	Roger	Josh	Mark	8/31/98	X		Misformed	1	Broken Quill	
Boulder	30826	2	Chris	Mike	Mike	8/31/98	X		Bump Height Out - high	1677		

A = Boulder Audit
C = Customer Concern

If reason is known and you can fill in a blank area as to what happened on a particular job, let Deb know!

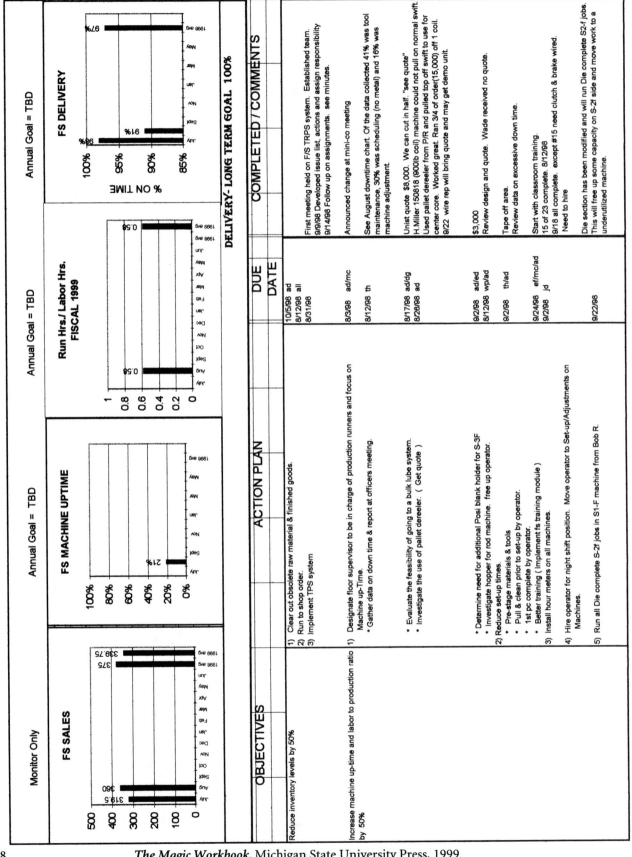

FS Cost - Fiscal 1999

Monitor Only — FS SALES

Annual Goal = TBD — FS MACHINE UPTIME — 21%

Annual Goal = TBD — Run Hrs./ Labor Hrs. FISCAL 1999 — 0.56 0.56

Annual Goal = TBD — FS DELIVERY — 96% 91% 97%
% ON TIME

DELIVERY - LONG TERM GOAL 100%

OBJECTIVES	ACTION PLAN	DUE DATE	COMPLETED / COMMENTS
Reduce inventory levels by 50%	1) Clear out obsolete raw material & finished goods. 2) Run to shop order. 3) Implement TPS system	10/5/98 ad 8/12/98 all 8/31/98	First meeting held on F/S TRPS system. Established team. 9/9/98 Developed issue list, actions and assign responsibility 9/14/98 Follow up on assignments. see minutes.
Increase machine up-time and labor to production ratio by 50%	1) Designate floor supervisor to be in charge of production runners and focus on Machine up-Time. * Gather data on down time & report at officers meeting.	8/3/98 ad/mc 8/12/98 th	Announced change at mini-co meeting See August downtime chart. Of the data collected 41% was tool maintenance, 30% was scheduling (no metal) and 16% was machine adjustment.
	* Evaluate the feasibility of going to a bulk lube system. * Investigate the use of pallet dereeler. (Get quote)	8/17/98 ad/dg 8/26/98 ad	Unist quote $8,000. We can cut in half. "see quote" H.Miller 150818 (800lb coil) machine could not pull on normal swift. Used pallet dereeler from P/R and pulled top off swift to use for center core. Worked great. Ran 3/4 of order(15,000) off 1 coil. 9/22 wire rep will bring quote and may get demo unit.
	* Determine need for additional Posi blank holder for S-3F * Investigate hopper for rod machine. free up operator. 2) Reduce set-up times. * Pre-stage materials & tools * Pull & clean prior to set-up by operator. * 1st pc complete by operator. * Better training (Implement fs training module) 3) Install hour meters on all machines.	9/2/98 ad/ed 8/12/98 wp/ad 9/2/98 th/ad 9/24/98 ef/mc/ad 9/2/98 jd	$3,000 Review design and quote. Wade received no quote. Tape off area. Review data on excessive down time. Start with classroom training. 15 of 23 complete. 8/12/98 9/18 all complete. except #15 need clutch & brake wired. Need to hire
	4) Hire operator for night shift position. Move operator to Set-up/Adjustments on Machines.		
	5) Run all Die complete S-2f jobs in S1-F machine from Bob R.	8/22/98	Die section has been modified and will run Die complete S2-f jobs. This will free up some capacity on S-2f side and move work to a underutilized machine.

FourSlide Downtime

Legend:
- ▨ Tool Maint
- ⊞ Scheduling
- Ⅲ Machine Adjust
- ▧ General Maint
- ☰ Communication
- ■ Machine
- ▨ Material
- ☐ Operations

Pie chart values: 41%, 30%, 16%, 4%, 3%, 3%, 2%, 1%

FS August DT by Machine

Bar chart machines (x-axis): 9, 2, 5, 14, 18, 12, 3, 7, 11, 15, 17, 10, 4, 13, 1 (y-axis 0–80)

August Reasons Detail	Hours
Not enough tolerance on slot dimension	.5
Piece of metal stuck in die	.75
Motor not turning on	1
2nd shift did not run enough parts	1
Coil needed changed	1
Die cleaned, Slugs in die	1.25
Cutter Blew	1.5
Fuse blew in machine	1.5
Swift broke	1.5
Material Buckle	2
Did not put die back into machine	2
Chute Problems	2
Timing Slipped	2
Lances uneven	2.25
Pin in die broke	2.5
Front Cam heating up	2.5
Die bed repaired	2.5
Machine and die maintenance	3.5
Material problems	3.5
Needed adjustment after 2nd changed coil	4
One tool sticking	4.5
Need ejector pins	5
Front tool getting wire burned	5
Post Broke	5.5
2nd shift did not know this was ready to run	7
Tool marks on parts	7.5
Adjustment Made	14.5
Punch broke, bent	20.5
Die trouble	60.25
No material	70
Total Downtime Hours for August (2 weeks)	**237.25**

NAI Charts

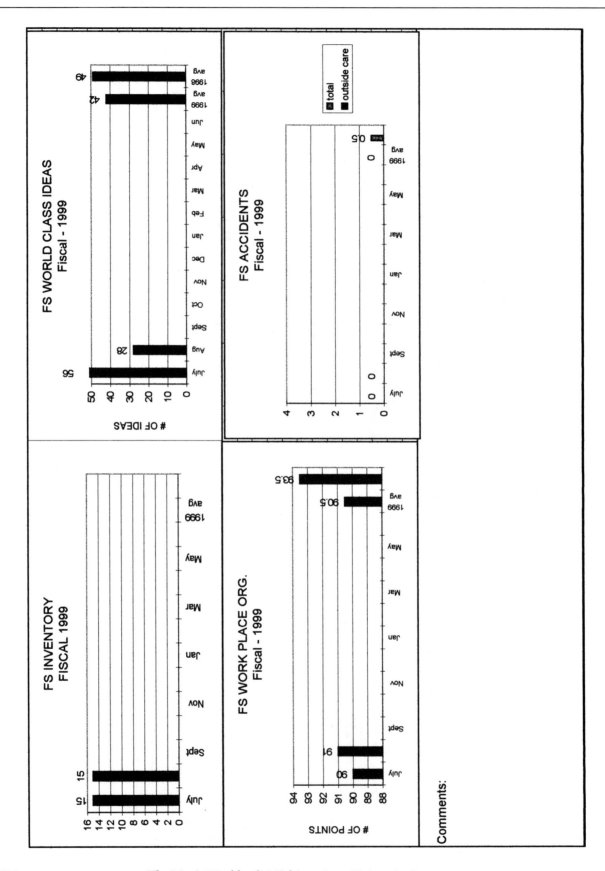

MAGIC INC.

EMPLOYEE SURVEY
DECEMBER 1995

	QUALITY	SECOND-ARY	FOUR-SLIDE	TOOL ROOM	ENG.	SPRING TORSION	SHIPPING /REC	PRESS ROOM	MAINT.	OFFICE	PLANT WIDE AVER. 1995	PLANT WIDE AVER. 1994
											4.42	4.4
1. Do you enjoy working at Magic?	4.86	4.50	4.23	4.31	4.43	4.42	4.44	4.38	4.33	4.50		4.08
2. Do you trust the management of the company? (includes supervisors)?	4.43	4.07	4.23	3.54	4.33	4.17	3.78	4.00	3.83	4.50	4.05	4.04
3. Do you like the mini-company concept?	4.43	4.00	4.23	3.69	3.86	3.92	2.33	3.88	3.67	3.83	3.80	3.97
4. Do you fully understand the concepts?	4.57	3.57	4.15	4.00	4.71	4.08	3.78	3.88	4.50	4.50	4.09	3.78
5. Have you been involved?	3.86	2.92	4.15	3.69	4.00	4.08	2.63	3.75	4.00	3.83	3.68	4.32
6. Have you seen improvements at Magic in the last year?	4.83	4.08	4.23	4.31	4.50	4.17	3.11	3.88	4.00	4.50	4.13	4.03
7. If so, did you like them?	4.33	4.00	4.17	3.92	4.33	4.08	3.80	3.86	4.17	4.17	4.07	3.88
8. Do you think lifelong training is important?	5.00	4.29	4.31	3.92	4.00	4.25	3.00	3.38	4.50	4.00	4.06	4.02
9. Should training be more technical?	3.57	3.83	4.00	3.92	4.71	4.17	4.11	3.75	3.83	3.83	3.98	3.02
10. Should training be more general?	2.86	3.25	2.92	2.77	2.57	2.50	1.89	3.00	2.83	2.60	2.74	3.81
11. Does it help you at Magic?	4.57	3.85	4.31	3.54	3.71	3.83	3.33	3.50	4.33	3.33	3.83	4.26
12. Have you contributed to the success of Magic in the last 12 months?	5.00	4.17	4.23	4.46	4.29	4.36	4.67	4.38	4.80	4.33	4.42	3.92
13. Could you have done more?	3.50	3.91	4.17	3.77	4.43	4.09	3.44	4.00	4.00	3.50	3.90	4.38
14. Will you contribute more in the next year?	4.83	4.17	4.58	4.08	4.71	4.58	4.33	4.25	5.00	4.00	4.42	4.16
15. Is this a safe place to work?	4.33	4.58	4.31	4.15	4.71	4.67	3.44	4.00	3.80	4.17	4.25	
16. Do you have any safety concerns?	2.83	2.50	2.15	2.45	2.57	2.25	3.33	2.75	3.00	2.33	2.56	Low is Good
THE NUMBER OF LOW SCORES BY DEPT.	0	1	2	2	1	0	7	3	1	1		
THE NUMBER OF HIGH SCORES BY DEPT.	7	1	2	0	2	1	0	0	2	2		
NUMBER OF PEOPLE WHO ANSWERED SURVEY	7	14	13	13	7	12	9	8	6	6	95 / 125 / 76%	

TOTAL EMPLOYEES
PERCENTAGE ANSWERED

CIRCLE = TWO LOWEST SCORES
SQUARE = TWO HIGHEST RESPONCES PER DEPARTMENT.
BLUE = NEITHER POSITIVE OR NEGATIVE
RED or CIRCLE = TWO LOWEST RESPONSES PER QUESTION

GREEN=LIFE LONG DOESN'T HELP IMPROVE OFFICE
PURPLE = CONTRIBUTED AS MUCH AS POSSIBLE, RESULTING IN LOW SCORE

SCALE: 5=DEFINATELY YES, 4=YES FOR THE MOST PART,
3=NEUTRAL, 2=NO FOR THE MOST PART,
1=DEFINATELY NO

Blending Quality Theories for Continuous Improvement

Grand Rapids Spring & Wire Products combines ideas of quality gurus to create a world-class competitor.

BY HARPER A. ROEHM, CPA;
DONALD KLEIN, CMA, AND
JOSEPH F. CASTELLANO

Certificate of Merit, 1993-94

As American companies strive to become competitive in a global economy, they are seeking the counsel and guidance of quality consultants who advocate the philosophies of such well known names as Deming, Juran, Schonberger, and Goldratt. While these philosophies do share some of the same underlying themes–a passion for quality and satisfying the customer–there are significant differences in their approaches that often make it extremely difficult for management to decide which approach to follow. In many instances executives who have received assistance from a particular consultant become strong disciples of the philosophy adopted. It is not that uncommon to have their organization referred to as a Deming, a Juran, a Goldratt, or a Schonberger company with the implication that there is only one approach to being competitive and achieving success.

Grand Rapids Spring & Wire Products Inc. (GRSW) is a company that has resisted such labeling in its efforts to become more customer focused and globally competitive. It has successfully blended many of the current quality philosophies and approaches and retained those ideas that the managers believe contribute to its flexibility and responsiveness in meeting customers' needs. The success of its approach provides a blueprint for other companies to consider.

GRSW SEEKS A QUALITY CULTURE

GRSW manufactures a variety of products that include compression, extension, and torsion springs; stampings from progressive dies and four-slide stampings; roll forming; wire and grommet molding; and various assembly processes. Approximately 70% of sales are to automotive companies with the other 30% to the appliance, furniture, and electronic industries. There are more than 1,000 spring companies in the United States and Canada with a total sales market of around $2 billion. It is a fragmented market in which no one company dominates.

Most spring manufacturing companies operate in a specific region. In the Western Michigan area GRSW has six competitors whose sales range from $1 million to $24 million and employ from 10 to 250 people. GRSW had 100 employees and sales of almost $12 million in 1992.

Jim Zawacki purchased Grand Rapids Spring & Wire Products Inc. (GRSW) in 1985 and immediately recognized the need to build a quality culture. He hired a statistical process control coordinator who prepared SPC materials and conducted SPC seminars for the employees. One of the largest customers requested that they study "world-class manufacturing" using Richard J. Schonberger's book, *Japanese Manufacturing Techniques: Nine Hidden Lessons in Simplicity*[1], and the accompanying videotapes. The book and its videotapes, which focus on "just-in-time" and "total quality control," were reviewed and studied by all employees. At the same time management and several of the employees were reading books about the Deming approach including W. Edwards Deming's *Out of the Crisis*[2].

THE GOLDRATT INFLUENCE

In 1987 GRSW hired a management consultantwho had been trained as a Jonah by Eliyahu M. Goldratt Institute. The consultant formed small employee groups who read *The Goal*[3] and discussed over a year how *The Goal* applied to GRSW. During these discussions the employees began to identify "Herbies" (constraints) which they felt were keeping GRSW from becoming a world-class manufacturer. As the discussions continued, management and the employees assisted each other in providing meaningful solutions to solving the identified constraints. As a result of these efforts GRSW was able to gain the trust and commitment of its employees.

When management took the initiative to listen and respond to employees, the workforce responded with an increased trust in management. As a result of this trust the quality culture began to flourish at GRSW. Although enormous progress had been achieved, Jim Zawacki, however, continued to search for new ideas and approaches to producing a quality product and to becoming even more committed to being flexible and responsive in meeting customers' needs.

SUZAKI INFLUENCE

After reading Kiyoshi Suzaki's book, *The New Manufacturing Challenge–Techniques for Contin-*

1 – MANAGEMENT ACCOUNTING/FEBRUARY 1995

*uous Improvement*⁴, which outlines the concept of creating mini-companies within a factory environment, Jim recommended that Kiyoshi Suzaki should be invited to speak to the Manufacturers Council of Grand Rapids Chamber of Commerce group. So impressed were they by his presentation that seven local companies formed a Continuous Improvement Users Group and hired Suzaki to visit and consult with them every six to eight weeks.

Eventually Jim hired Suzaki as a consultant to GRSW. The idea of creating mini-companies within a factory had great appeal because it focused on having each employee assume ownership of his or her work. Theoretically each person could be considered president of his own company within the company because each person has internal and external suppliers and customers. Employees rarely work in isolation and usually either receive information, services, or products from someone either internal or external to the company who would be considered their supplier.

Furthermore they usually provide either information, services, or products to someone either internal or external to the company who would be considered their customer. If each person's job is viewed as a separate mini-company that has both suppliers and customers, each person would be responsible for his own supplier relations and for understanding the needs of his customers. At the same time, each person would be both a supplier and a customer. In addition, as a president of a company, each person would be responsible for providing for solutions to problems and the implementation of those solutions. This approach promotes a strategy of addressing problems at their source and allows employees a better opportunity to use their experience and innovation for better serving the final customer of the company.

FORMATION OF MINI-COMPANIES

Initially GRSW formed 11 mini-companies. In an attempt to create cross-functional, self-directed units that would enhance continuous improvement, it assigned each mini-company support people—accountants, engineers, marketing people, toolmakers, and quality experts. After one year, however, managers found that the support people were unable to devote sufficient time to each unit. As a result they reduced the number to the four units that generate throughput–Small Metal Stamping, Four-Slide Stamping, Spring Torsion, and Secondary. Each mini-company was assigned a person from accounting, engineering, marketing quality, toolmaking, shipping, and general administration who attends mini-company meetings. The general manager and the plant manager each attend the meetings of two mini-companies. This new organization has created a much flatter structure and has improved communications.

Each mini-company has three officers who are equally responsible for developing a vision, a mission, and a business plan that is approved by the president, the general manager, and the plant manager.

Continuous improvement directed towards customer satisfaction is the heart of the Secondary Mini-Company's vision and mission statement. The letters Q C D S M represent *quality, cost, delivery, safety,* and *morale* and are what Suzaki feels are central to addressing customer needs and customer satisfaction. He states:

"In other words if we can satisfy our customers continuously with high quality (Q) products or services, at less cost (C), and with shorter and more time delivery (D) than competitors, we should do well.... Also, since all employ-

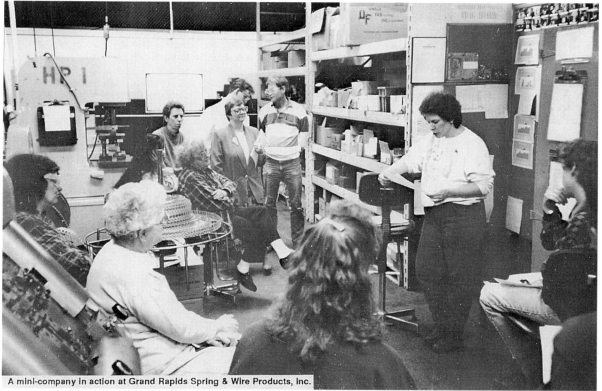

A mini-company in action at Grand Rapids Spring & Wire Products, Inc.

MANAGEMENT ACCOUNTING/FEBRUARY 1995 – 2

ees in the organization can be viewed as customers from the total company's point of view, their needs must be satisfied. Therefore, if we add safety (S) and morale (M) to address employee concerns, QCDSM become the major criteria for an organization's success."[5]

The business plan follows the vision and mission statements with some very specific actions as to how the vision and mission will be accomplished. For each action the plan delineates who is responsible, when it is to be accomplished, and how it is to be accomplished with space left for comments. Color coding is used to indicate the status of each action, and symbols are used to indicate how strong, medium, or weak the action plan's relationship is to QCDSM.

For example, the first action listed in the plan is: Integrate weld information into computer system. Who: Ross, Barb, and Randy are responsible. How: Jeff Dennis is to teach them. This particular action has a strong relationship to quality, a medium relationship to both cost and morale, a weak relationship to delivery, and no relationship to safety. The light green color indicates that the achievement of this action is progressing faster than originally scheduled.

Each mini-factory prepares process flow diagrams for each customer product.

Each employee must have a complete understanding of all processes in his or her mini-company in order to be able to solve problems as they arise and be capable of offering continuous improvement suggestions. The process flow diagrams are an essential ingredient in providing this understanding and are placed at the site of each mini-factory where each employee has easy access. Key performance indicators for each

mini-factory process have been developed to measure quality, cost, delivery, safety, and morale.

The quality indicators include defective parts per million (PPM) where 200 is considered the goal. The 38,701 figure (a completed lot that was rejected) in January is marked in red to indicate that it has exceeded the limit and has a major problem. The next quality indicator is capability process index (CPK) which measures the amount of the process tolerances you are statistically using. An acceptable performance for the CPK is considered anything greater than 1.5. While 1.37 for March is unacceptable, it is much closer to 1.5, and, therefore, the 1.37 is marked in blue to indicate improvement. Once an acceptable level of performance is reached, the numbers are recorded in green. The other quality indicators include .5% for returns and allowances and 2 for registered customer concerns. Anytime a process fails to achieve an indicator's predetermined performance measure a team is formed to define and solve the problem.

The mini-company employees meet with their support people each week to review the progress on QCDS and M and their key performance indicators. The mini-company officers meet on an ad hoc basis as needed; however, they meet with what they refer to as the internal bankers (the president, general manager, and plant manager) once a month to review the overall performance and make requests for additional funding for such things as training and equipment. Twice a year the company holds a stakeholder's meeting for all employees where they review how the mini-company is progressing toward its vision, mission, and business plan. Each mini-company is responsible for its presentation

and is encouraged to prepare and use visual aids such as films and slides.

THE BLENDING OF IDEAS

The blending of quality experts' ideas occurs in a number of ways. Three examples will be illustrated. The first example occurs in determining specific actions to be accomplished in the business plan. The second deals with how employees go about solving problems that are indicated by the "Key Performance Indicator" report. The last example illustrates how GRSW has attempted to tie Suzaki's performance indicators to Goldratt's accounting model and Goldratt's model to the traditional income statement and balance sheet.

While Kiyoshi Suzaki's mini-company concept has dominated GRSW for the past several years, GRSW has used many of the ideas learned from other quality experts to implement the mini-company.

For example, after writing vision and mission statements for each mini-factory, it used the "Herbie" process that had been developed while implementing E. Goldratt's "theory of constraints" where groups of employees identify which constraints are preventing them (in this case the mini-company) from achieving their mission and vision. The business plan for the Secondary Mini-Company illustrates how the employees of this particular mini-company are attempting to eliminate their constraints. The first action recommended, "Integrate weld information into computer," arose because customers were demanding some assurance as to the pushout strength of welds and it was impossible to accomplish the analysis to the customer's satisfaction without a computer.

The third action of the plan states "Rearrange department for improved productivity and information flow." The employees felt intuitively that if they could examine these areas as a group they could improve both productivity and information flow. The "how" for this action–"Brainstorm with Department"– reflects the success of the Goldratt technique with previous quality initiatives. They intend to "brainstorm" with all of the employees. In effect, they are signaling management that they are capable of improving the production and information flow by using their own talent and creativity.

Furthermore, management is more than willing to allow them to attempt

Barb Rowe, Tom Vickers, Rose Witte, Mini-company Secondary Officers

3 – MANAGEMENT ACCOUNTING/FEBRUARY 1995

such action. These attitudes reflect the trust and confidence that each group has in the other as a result of the successful implementation of other quality programs, in particular the Goldratt approach. Finally, the fifth action of the plan requires the use of Pareto analysis, a technique taught earlier while implementing the "Herbie" process.

The second example of how GRSW has blended various quality experts' approaches is found in the technique used to solve problems. A story board illustrates a method for solving a specific problem that came to its attention when returns and allowances on Suzaki's Key Performance Indicators report was recorded at .6%, indicating that a possible problem might exist.

The mini-company uses an expanded version of Dr. W. Edwards Deming's Cycle of Plan, Do, Check, and Act. It first determined that the customer with the problem was XYZ (although the name has been changed, the facts have not been altered). Next, the mini-company defined the situation (problem) as: A. Plating, B. Loose grommets, and C. Bent tabs. Number 2, Current Situation, explains how it identified the source of the problems. The team used data collection sheets and flowcharts and visited the platers where they inspected and sorted 1,800 pieces after the process, 1,000 pieces off the process, and 100% after the second operation.

Finally, the team studied all of these parts, and, from this study, it attempted to analyze the causes that are summarized in #3. Analyze causes. It concluded that the handling at the platers and their packaging of the parts were the most probable causes of the bent tabs and that the most likely source of the loose grommets was the die not bottoming out every time. Team members listed their recommended solutions to these problems in #4. Try out improvement/solution. To correct the bent tab problem they are recommending that a #23 box be used for packaging. They are recommending that new lubricants be used and that a limit switch/timer be installed on the second press to eliminate loose grommets. As of now, the study results listed in box #5 indicate that the bent tab problem has been corrected but they are still finding loose grommets.

The team will continue this process until the problem is solved and it is able to make a presentation and celebrate as indicated in box #8. The Deming Cycle of Plan, Do, Check, and Act is a critical part of the mini-company team's continuous improvement effort to meet customers' needs.

As our final example, GRSW is integrating Suzaki's performance indicators with Goldratt's measurements and traditional financial statements. Figure 5 illustrates how the company believes Suzaki, Goldratt, and traditional financial statements can be integrated.

The individual performance indicators for quality, cost, delivery, safety, and morale are the central measurements used by Suzaki. Goldratt defines (T) throughput as the rate at which the business generates money through sales; (OE) operating expenses as all the money that the system spends in turning inventory and services into throughput; and (I) inventory/investment as all the money that the system invests in purchasing items and services the system intends to sell. Net income is defined as (T) throughput minus (OE) operating expenses; return on investment (ROI) as throughput minus operating expenses divided by investment; productivity of operations (income statement) as (T) throughput divided by (OE) operating expenses; and, finally, productivity of capital (balance sheet) as (T) throughput divided by (I) investment.

In 1987 the GRSW employees were taught that if throughput is increased, or operating expenses decreased, or investment decreased while at the same time holding the other variables constant, the overall "goal" of making money would be achieved. This accounting model became more useful and operational for employees than the traditional accounting-based targets. It was much easier for the plant personnel to relate what they were doing to improve the process to the T, I, and OE measurements. Suzaki's performance measurements, which were introduced in 1990, became even more factory-floor specific. As a result, Suzaki's measurements are more useful in determining what operational issues need to be addressed for continuous improvement.

GRSW's attempt to integrate the various models is shown. If defective parts per million are reduced along with returns and allowances, throughput will be increased and income improved. However, not all relationships are as clear. For example, if the number of implemented ideas is increased they know that morale will be higher and, as a result, operating expenses may be reduced. It is also possible that invest-ment may be reduced and throughput increased. A diagram helps employees to understand how their actions relate to the key performance indicators used by GRSW. GRSW also believes that this approach is helping it to maintain and strengthen its financial performance. Jim believes that GRSW's focus should be on Q (Quality), C (Cost), D (Delivery), S (Safety), and M (Morale) and not on the bottom line.

RESULT: A LEARNING ORGANIZATION

GRSW successfully has blended the quality initiatives of Dr. W. Edwards Deming, Dr. Eliyahu M. Goldratt, and, most recently, Kiyoshi Suzaki. As a result of its efforts to create a quality culture, it has achieved the reputation of being a globally competitive world-class manufacturer. By successfully integrating key elements of the quality philosophies noted above, Jim Zawaki not only has established the foundation needed for continuous improvement and customer satisfaction but also has transformed GRSW into a learning organization. In the final analysis, this may be GRSW's most sustainable competitive advantage. ∎

Harper A. Roehm, CPA, DBA, is professor of accounting, the University of Dayton, Dayton, Ohio. He is a member of the Dayton Chapter, through which this article was submitted. He can be reached at (513) 229-2497.

Donald Klein, CPA, CMA, DBA, is professor of accounting, Grand Valley State University, Grand Rapids, Mich.

Joseph F. Castellano, Ph.D., is professor of accountancy, Wright State University, Dayton, Ohio. He is a member of the Dayton Chapter.

EMPLOYEE SURVEY

We believe that an annual employee survey is a technique that keeps us in touch with what our associates are thinking. Each December we meet and discuss the survey with them for about fifteen minutes before they actually complete it. We share the purpose of the survey, encourage associates to be truthful, and give them an opportunity to ask any question about the survey or anything else. Nothing is sacred—from pay to the organization of the company. They privately respond to the survey during the balance of the hour. Associates must identify their department, because different departments might have different issues. Whether or not they sign their name is up to them.

The surveys are tabulated and analyzed for ways to improve our company. The internal bankers associated with the mini-company structure meet with each department to discuss the results. This direct communication not only brings clarity to many perception gaps, but provides management an opportunity to communicate its thinking and learn more about the items on the survey that did not score as well as management would like. The survey indirectly measures our morale. The nature of the responses to the questions, failure to respond to last year's valid criticism, and our face-to-face dialogue provide a sense of how people in the company feel.

Attached is a tabulated summary of an employee survey. We focus more on the lowest scores for each department and for the company as a whole. For example, on the 1996 survey we found a company wide low score for general training [2.74]. This caught our attention. We found out that employees wanted more specific skills training.

We also look to see if a department has a large number of low scores. In 1996 the pressroom had seven of the lowest scores out of eighteen possible. This alerted us to the need to more fully explore with this department the concerns they have.

Responses vary from high praise to complaints that "you don't do enough." The response that pleases us the most is the high score for "Do you like working here?" The statement that "little things mean a lot" goes a long way in improving morale. Our survey provides a way to discuss little as well as large things.

MAGIC INC.

EMPLOYEE SURVEY
DECEMBER 1995

	QUALITY	SECOND-ARY	FOUR-SLIDE	TOOL ROOM	ENG.	SPRING TORSION	SHIPPING /REC	PRESS ROOM	MAINT.	OFFICE	PLANT WIDE AVER. 1995	PLANT WIDE AVER. 1994
1. Do you enjoy working at Magic?	4.86	4.50	4.23	4.31	4.43	4.42	4.44	4.38	4.33	4.50	4.42	4.4
2. Do you trust the management of the company? (includes supervisors)?	4.43	4.07	4.23	3.54	4.33	4.17	3.78	4.00	3.83	4.50	4.05	4.08
3. Do you like the mini-company concept?	4.43	4.00	4.23	3.69	3.86	3.92	2.33	3.88	3.67	3.83	3.80	4.04
4. Do you fully understand the concepts?	4.57	3.57	4.15	4.00	4.71	4.08	3.78	3.88	4.50	4.50	4.09	3.97
5. Have you been involved?	3.86	2.92	4.15	3.69	4.00	4.08	2.63	3.75	4.00	3.83	3.68	3.78
6. Have you seen improvements at Magic in the last year?	4.83	4.08	4.23	4.31	4.50	4.17	3.11	3.88	4.00	4.50	4.13	4.32
7. If so, did you like them?	4.33	4.00	4.17	3.92	4.33	4.08	3.80	3.86	4.17	4.17	4.07	4.03
8. Do you think lifelong training is important?	5.00	4.29	4.31	3.92	4.00	4.25	3.00	3.38	4.50	4.00	4.06	3.88
9. Should training be more technical?	3.57	3.83	4.00	3.92	4.71	4.17	4.11	3.75	3.83	3.83	3.98	4.02
10. Should training be more general?	2.86	3.25	2.92	2.77	2.57	2.50	1.89	3.00	2.83	2.60	2.74	3.02
11. Does it help you at Magic?	4.57	3.85	4.31	3.54	3.71	3.83	3.33	3.50	4.33	3.33	3.83	3.81
12. Have you contributed to the success of Magic in the last 12 months?	5.00	4.17	4.23	4.46	4.29	4.36	4.67	4.38	4.80	4.33	4.42	4.26
13. Could you have done more?	3.50	3.91	4.17	3.77	4.43	4.09	3.44	4.00	4.00	3.50	3.90	3.92
14. Will you contribute more in the next year?	4.83	4.17	4.58	4.08	4.71	4.58	4.33	4.25	5.00	4.00	4.42	4.38
15. Is this a safe place to work?	4.33	4.58	4.31	4.15	4.71	4.67	3.44	4.00	3.80	4.17	4.25	4.16
16. Do you have any safety concerns?	2.83	2.50	2.15	2.45	2.57	2.25	3.33	2.75	3.00	2.33	2.56	Low is Good
THE NUMBER OF LOW SCORES BY DEPT.	0	1	2	2	1	0	7	3	1	1		
THE NUMBER OF HIGH SCORES BY DEPT.	7	1	2	0	2	1	0	0	2	2		
NUMBER OF PEOPLE WHO ANSWERED SURVEY	7	14	13	13	7	12	9	8	6	6		

TOTAL EMPLOYEES 95
125
PERCENTAGE ANSWERED 76%

CIRCLE = TWO LOWEST SCORES
SQUARE = TWO HIGHEST RESPONCES PER DEPARTMENT.
BLUE = NEITHER POSITIVE OR NEGATIVE   GREEN=LIFE LONG DOESN'T HELP IMPROVE OFFICE
RED or CIRCLE = TWO LOWEST RESPONSES PER QUESTION   PURPLE = CONTRIBUTED AS MUCH AS POSSIBLE, RESULTING IN LOW SCORE

SCALE: 5=DEFINATELY YES, 4=YES FOR THE MOST PART,
3=NEUTRAL, 2=NO FOR THE MOST PART,
1=DEFINATELY NO

PRESS TEAM QUALITY OF WORKLIFE SURVEY
_____Quarter:_____

Rating Scale: 1=Bad, 2=Poor, 3=Just OK, 4=Good, 5=Excellent

	1	2	3	4	5
Clear Company Direction Comments	1	2	3	4	5
Clear Press Team Direction Comments:	1	2	3	4	5
Press Team Focused on projects supporting CI Objectives Comments:	1	2	3	4	5
Team Leader support for your team Comments:	1	2	3	4	5
Cooperative spirit within press team Comments:	1	2	3	4	5
Feeling of trust among press team members Comments:	1	2	3	4	5
Fair treatment of personnel issues Comments:	1	2	3	4	5
Good work environment (physical setting) Comments:	1	2	3	4	5
Appropriate resources/tools to do job Comments:	1	2	3	4	5
Fair compensation Comments:	1	2	3	4	5
Clear understanding of benefits & their value (insurance, 401K, FSA, etc.) Comments:	1	2	3	4	5
Balance of work and family life Comments:	1	2	3	4	5
Opportunity for personal growth and advancement Comments:	1	2	3	4	5
Challenging and satisfying work Comments:	1	2	3	4	5
Feeling empowered to carry out responsibilities Comments:	1	2	3	4	5
SUMMARY RATING	1	2	3	4	5

Other comments: other categories to add

TRIBAL HISTORY

It is important to know who you are, where you have been, and what you have accomplished. We refer to this kind of information as a history of our company family or tribe. Our history takes the form of visual, oral, and written communications about the major events, both good and bad, in the life of the organization. We believe that preserving and celebrating our tribal history creates pride and a sense of ownership.

One day years ago, the president (Peter) of Magic finished a roll of film by taking pictures of some of the associates at Magic. He put the associates' pictures on the information board, and many people noticed and remarked on them. So Peter started taking more pictures of people doing a variety of things at the company—people working, participating in cultural events, involved in education programs, posing with visitors, at the company picnic, and so on. A quarterly collage showing each worker's face at least once was hung in a high traffic area. It was amazing how many associates and guests paused to look at the pictures. In the center of all the many pictures was a date and theme of the major event that had occurred in that quarter. Today there are cameras at various locations throughout the company and everyone is encouraged to photograph "Kodak" moments. Once the roll of film is completed, it is turned into the office for replacement and processing.

Today we have a standard size frame for the collages and have used some simple grooved wood trim to hold over forty collages. We make sure that each collage contains each associate's face at least once. Walking down collage lane shows not only the history of the major events of the company, but also records all the associates who have helped build the company. Many positive memories are relived from these pictures. The pictures vividly remind everyone of the many changes that the company has made, but they also remind us that our history is the story of who we are.

We also celebrate our history by posting our corporate scoreboard, which records quality, cost, delivery, safety, and morale, portrayed with graphs and charts.

These are ways of letting associates take pride in their accomplishments. Our tribal history educates new associates and lets them appreciate and understand the company's past. The various accomplishments help to increase morale and self-esteem. More important, our history helps us remember the obstacles we've overcome and reminds us that together we can become even better.

COLLAGE

CULTURE, FAMILY,
T.R.I.C &
Q.C.D.S.M

The Magic Workbook, Michigan State University Press, 1999

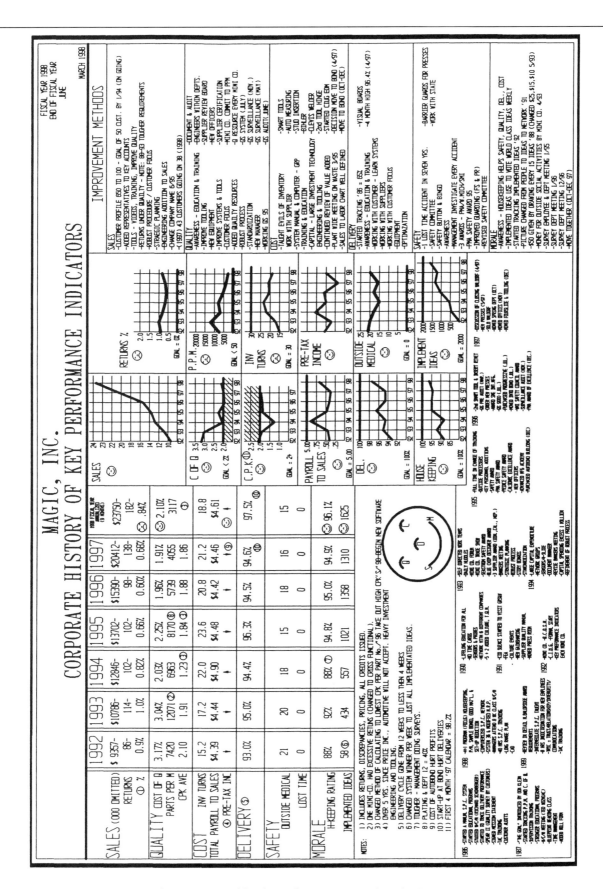

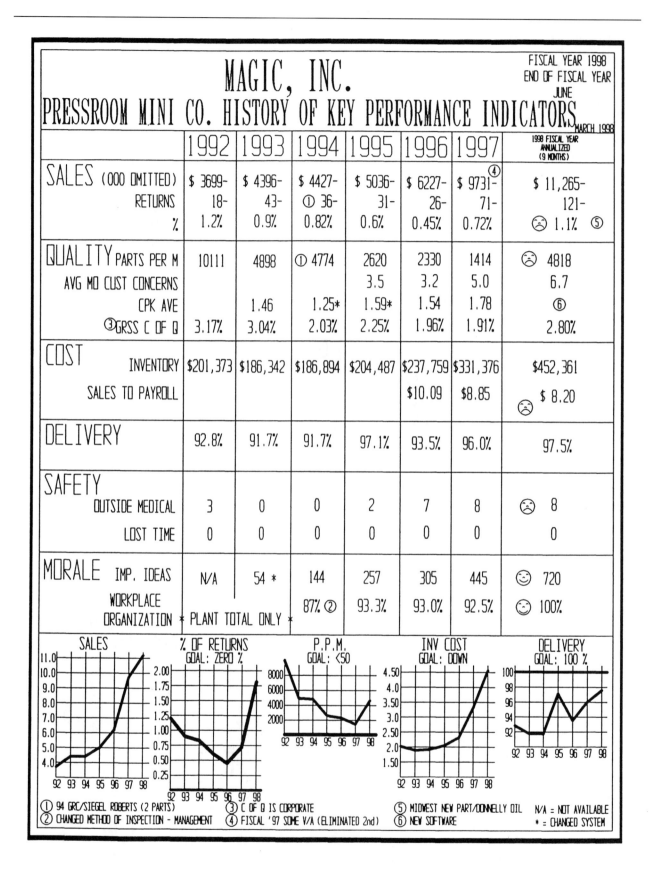

MAGIC, INC.
PRESSROOM MINI CO. HISTORY OF KEY PERFORMANCE INDICATORS

FISCAL YEAR 1998
END OF FISCAL YEAR
JUNE
MARCH 1998

	1992	1993	1994	1995	1996	1997	1998 FISCAL YEAR ANNUALIZED (9 MONTHS)
SALES (000 OMITTED)	$ 3699-	$ 4396-	$ 4427-	$ 5036-	$ 6227-	$ 9731- ④	$ 11,265-
RETURNS	18-	43-	① 36-	31-	26-	71-	121-
%	1.2%	0.9%	0.82%	0.6%	0.45%	0.72%	☹ 1.1% ⑤
QUALITY PARTS PER M	10111	4898	① 4774	2620	2330	1414	☹ 4818
AVG MO CUST CONCERNS				3.5	3.2	5.0	6.7
CPK AVE		1.46	1.25*	1.59*	1.54	1.78	⑥
③ GRSS C OF Q	3.17%	3.04%	2.03%	2.25%	1.96%	1.91%	2.80%
COST INVENTORY	$201,373	$186,342	$186,894	$204,487	$237,759	$331,376	$452,361
SALES TO PAYROLL					$10.09	$8.85	☹ $ 8.20
DELIVERY	92.8%	91.7%	91.7%	97.1%	93.5%	96.0%	97.5%
SAFETY OUTSIDE MEDICAL	3	0	0	2	7	8	☹ 8
LOST TIME	0	0	0	0	0	0	0
MORALE IMP. IDEAS	N/A	54 *	144	257	305	445	☺ 720
WORKPLACE ORGANIZATION	* PLANT TOTAL ONLY *		87% ②	93.3%	93.0%	92.5%	☺ 100%

SALES

% OF RETURNS
GOAL: ZERO %

P.P.M.
GOAL: <50

INV COST
GOAL: DOWN

DELIVERY
GOAL: 100 %

① 94 GRC/SIEGEL ROBERTS (2 PARTS)
② CHANGED METHOD OF INSPECTION - MANAGEMENT
③ C OF Q IS CORPORATE
④ FISCAL '97 SOME V/A (ELIMINATED 2nd)
⑤ MIDWEST NEW PART/DONNELLY OIL
⑥ NEW SOFTWARE
N/A = NOT AVAILABLE
* = CHANGED SYSTEM

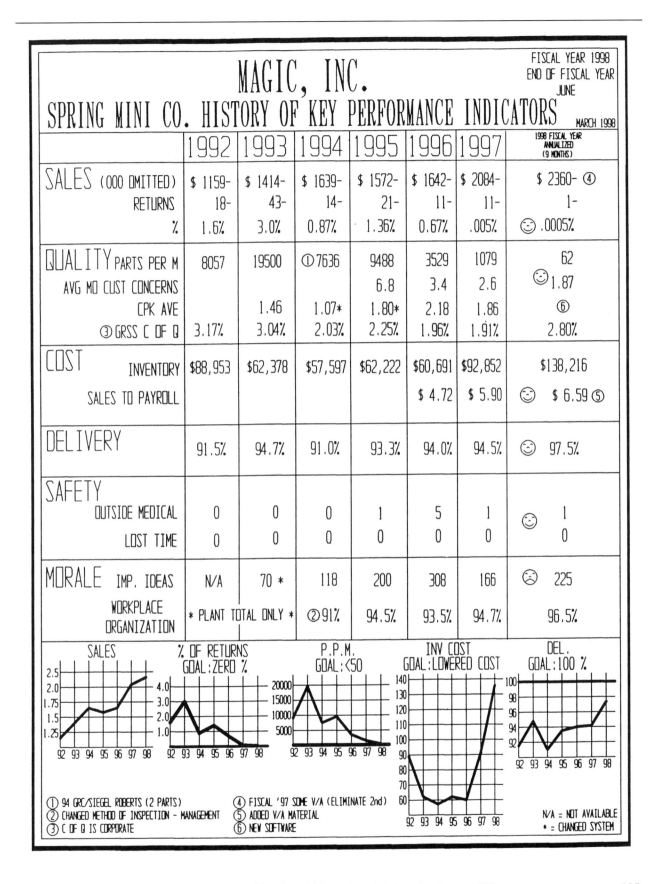

MAGIC, INC.

FISCAL YEAR 1998
END OF FISCAL YEAR
JUNE

SPRING MINI CO. HISTORY OF KEY PERFORMANCE INDICATORS

MARCH 1998

	1992	1993	1994	1995	1996	1997	1998 FISCAL YEAR ANNUALIZED (9 MONTHS)
SALES (000 OMITTED)	$ 1159-	$ 1414-	$ 1639-	$ 1572-	$ 1642-	$ 2084-	$ 2360- ④
RETURNS	18-	43-	14-	21-	11-	11-	1-
%	1.6%	3.0%	0.87%	1.36%	0.67%	.005%	☺ .0005%
QUALITY PARTS PER M	8057	19500	① 7636	9488	3529	1079	62
AVG MO CUST CONCERNS				6.8	3.4	2.6	☺ 1.87
CPK AVE		1.46	1.07*	1.80*	2.18	1.86	⑥
③ GRSS C OF Q	3.17%	3.04%	2.03%	2.25%	1.96%	1.91%	2.80%
COST INVENTORY	$88,953	$62,378	$57,597	$62,222	$60,691	$92,852	$138,216
SALES TO PAYROLL					$ 4.72	$ 5.90	☺ $ 6.59 ⑤
DELIVERY	91.5%	94.7%	91.0%	93.3%	94.0%	94.5%	☺ 97.5%
SAFETY OUTSIDE MEDICAL	0	0	0	1	5	1	☺ 1
LOST TIME	0	0	0	0	0	0	0
MORALE IMP. IDEAS	N/A	70 *	118	200	308	166	☹ 225
WORKPLACE ORGANIZATION	* PLANT TOTAL ONLY *		② 91%	94.5%	93.5%	94.7%	96.5%

SALES

% OF RETURNS GOAL: ZERO %

P.P.M. GOAL: <50

INV COST GOAL: LOWERED COST

DEL. GOAL: 100 %

① 94 GRC/SIEGEL ROBERTS (2 PARTS)
② CHANGED METHOD OF INSPECTION - MANAGEMENT
③ C OF Q IS CORPORATE
④ FISCAL '97 SOME V/A (ELIMINATE 2nd)
⑤ ADDED V/A MATERIAL
⑥ NEW SOFTWARE

N/A = NOT AVAILABLE
* = CHANGED SYSTEM

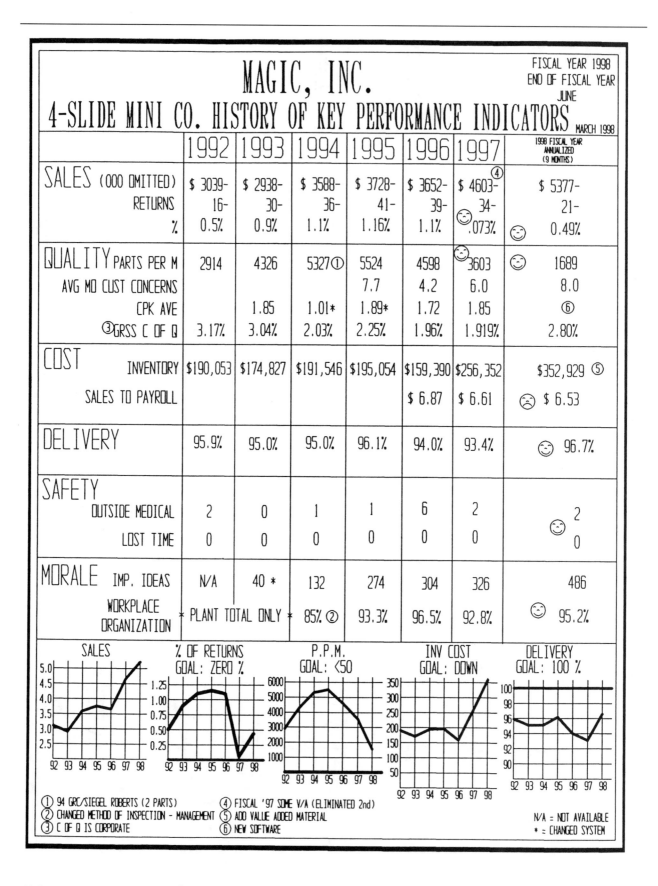

MAGIC, INC.

4-SLIDE MINI CO. HISTORY OF KEY PERFORMANCE INDICATORS

	1992	1993	1994	1995	1996	1997	1998 FISCAL YEAR ANNUALIZED (9 MONTHS)
SALES (000 OMITTED)	$ 3039-	$ 2938-	$ 3588-	$ 3728-	$ 3652-	$ 4603- ④	$ 5377-
RETURNS	16-	30-	36-	41-	39-	34- ☺	21-
%	0.5%	0.9%	1.1%	1.16%	1.1%	.073%	☺ 0.49%
QUALITY PARTS PER M	2914	4326	5327 ①	5524	4598	☺ 3603	☺ 1689
AVG MO CUST CONCERNS				7.7	4.2	6.0	8.0
CPK AVE		1.85	1.01*	1.89*	1.72	1.85	⑥
③ GRSS C OF Q	3.17%	3.04%	2.03%	2.25%	1.96%	1.919%	2.80%
COST INVENTORY	$190,053	$174,827	$191,546	$195,054	$159,390	$256,352	$352,929 ⑤
SALES TO PAYROLL					$ 6.87	$ 6.61	☹ $ 6.53
DELIVERY	95.9%	95.0%	95.0%	96.1%	94.0%	93.4%	☺ 96.7%
SAFETY OUTSIDE MEDICAL	2	0	1	1	6	2	☺ 2
LOST TIME	0	0	0	0	0	0	0
MORALE IMP. IDEAS	N/A	40 *	132	274	304	326	486
WORKPLACE ORGANIZATION	* PLANT TOTAL ONLY *		85% ②	93.3%	96.5%	92.8%	☺ 95.2%

SALES	% OF RETURNS GOAL: ZERO %	P.P.M. GOAL: <50	INV COST GOAL: DOWN	DELIVERY GOAL: 100 %

① 94 GRC/SIEGEL ROBERTS (2 PARTS) ④ FISCAL '97 SOME V/A (ELIMINATED 2nd)
② CHANGED METHOD OF INSPECTION - MANAGEMENT ⑤ ADD VALUE ADDED MATERIAL
③ C OF Q IS CORPORATE ⑥ NEW SOFTWARE

N/A = NOT AVAILABLE
* = CHANGED SYSTEM

The Magic Workbook, Michigan State University Press, 1999

MAGIC, INC.

VALUE ADDED MINI CO. HISTORY OF KEY PERFORMANCE INDICATORS

MARCH 1998

	1992	1993	1994	1995	1996	1997	1998 FISCAL YEAR ANNUALIZED (9 MONTHS)
SALES (000 OMITTED)	$ 640-	$ 695-	$ 925-	$ 1220-	$ 1320-	③	③
RETURNS	4-	4-	3-	5-	△ 5-		
%	0.6%	0.6%	0.39%	0.4%	0.42%		
QUALITY PARTS PER M	7626	1379	0	④1800	1793	③	22
AVG MO CUST CONCERNS				1.7	1.3		☺ 1.7
CPK AVE		1.88	1.50*	2.11*	2.07		③
②GRSS C OF Q	3.17%	3.04%	2.03%	2.25%	1.96%		2.80%
COST INVENTORY	$27371	$39695	$47585	$61166	$59811	③	③
SALES TO PAYROLL					$ 4.37		
DELIVERY	95.9%	98.6%	99.0%	98.0%	99.5%	③	③
SAFETY OUTSIDE MEDICAL	0	0	0	2	0	③	2
LOST TIME	0	0	0	0	0		0
MORALE IMP. IDEAS	N/A	32 *	124	195	271	③	200 ☺
WORKPLACE ORGANIZATION	* PLANT TOTAL ONLY *		96% ①	93.3%	100%		99.3%

N/A = NOT AVAILABLE
* = CHANGED SYSTEM
△ = ROLLFORM = 98%

① CHANGED METHOD OF INSPECTION - MANAGEMENT
② C OF Q IS CORPORATE
③ STATISTICS CALCULATED IN ORIGINATING DEPARTMENTS (97,98)
④ END R.J. TOWER & OIL ROLL FORM

SALES ☺   % OF RETURNS ☺   P.P.M. ☺   INV COST ☺   DEL. ☺

VERNACULAR

If you don't focus on the weakest link of your organization (a chain), all other efforts have little effect on strengthening it. We have learned that developing a small but meaningful vernacular helps everyone focus on the weakest links. To that end, we used some of the key words from *The Goal*. Some of the words are:

CONSTRAINT: Anything that limits the system from meeting a higher performance relative to its goal. This is also known as a "Herbie." (See chapter 19.)

NONCONSTRAINT: All other resources that are not the constraint.

BOTTLENECK: A bottleneck is a resource that cannot meet or exceed market demand. You can have ninety-nine bottlenecks, but the one that holds you back the most is the constraint bottleneck. Focus there to get the most benefit for your limited amount of time, energy, and resources.

THROUGHPUT: The rate at which the system generates money through sales.

OPERATING EXPENSE: All the money the system spends in turning inventory into throughput.

INVENTORY/INVESTMENT: All the money the system invests in purchasing things the system intends to sell.

We also developed some of our own expressions:

FOLLOW THROUGH versus FALL THROUGH: Are we getting things done or are we allowing things to fall through the cracks?

OVER and OVER: We need to remind people and train them over and over. People usually don't listen or comprehend the message the first time, so many times we need to repeat the lesson. However, there is a limit as to how many over and overs are reasonable.

VERBALIZE: This word means that I am going to ramble for a while and you should help me out if you can. It also means that I have an idea but am not sure where it might take me or us. It is a freedom word just to speak out and see what comes of the comments.

KILL versus WOUND: Kill means to put the problem out of its misery once and for all. The problem will never come back again. Wound means to place a Band-Aid on the problem instead of permanently eliminating it.

HOLD THAT GAIN: Once we have successfully implemented a positive change we don't want associates to slip back into old habits. So we remind each other to "hold the gain."

We also use stories to make points as well as brief little statements to help us remember key things. Most individuals remember stories more easily than commands and the message that goes with them.

Two we use are:

Don't let perfect get in the way of better: Start now and do something on the never-ending journey of continuous improvement.

By the inch it is a cinch and by the yard it is hard: Take little steps and they will get you where you want to go.

We suggest that you start recording the key expressions that convey the concepts you want your associates to remember and use. Then use them often. Teach them to new employees during orientation. Whenever we read or hear of a new expression we think will help us, we put it into use and retain it. A simple and easy to remember set of words, expressions, and stories helps a company stay focused on its goals and increases the clarity of communication. The community that speaks the same language can move united toward the same goals.

Customer Profile

Some customers will not help your organization grow. Sometimes you need to optimize a few customers in order to better manage your resources. It is important to optimize your customer base. By examining the attached exhibit, you can see some of the attributes that make it easier for us to manage and for our associates to be productive. Our customers should be financially stable and willing to go into partnership with us. In addition, we ask ourselves, can this customer take us to new heights and introduce us to new technologies? After all, we are going to experience our life in the future and not in the past.

- Our direct salespeople and our sales representatives must describe in writing how a potential customer stacks up against each of the attributes we have identified as key to our success. Any exceptions must be presented and debated. Yearly we assess our existing customers against the attribute list. We discuss any major changes and take appropriate action. Sometimes we decide a certain customer is not for us. More often we decide to grow closer to the customer by spending more time with the right people, the key decision makers in the process.

- We review our activities and relationships during our quarterly strategic planning reviews. The attached exhibits indicate the types of forms we use to help us assess our customer base.
- It is easier and more effective to develop relationships with twenty organizations than one hundred. How many additional calls, personalities, quality issues, different systems, and so forth are required by a larger customer base? We are working diligently to grow with the customers who will make us a better organization. We have decreased our customer base from over six hundred to forty in ten years, while at the same time sales have tripled. We plan to reduce it even further. It becomes exceedingly more challenging and constructive to optimize your customer list once you purge the ones that give you little business, low margins, and have no interest in a partnership over time.

Today we are learning to use competitive intelligence techniques from the world wide web. We have more data available today in the public domain about existing and potential customers than ever before, which only makes it more desirable to find and concentrate on the customers who are right for you.

MAGIC, INC.

CUSTOMER PROFILE

1. Financially strong.
   - Ability to pay.

2. Partnership orientation with suppliers.

3. Leader in their industry/segment.

4. Good cultural fit.

5. Global orientation.

6. Overall business potential.

7. Can learn from them.

8. Key markets - Automotive/Appliance/Communications/Computers/Office Furniture.

9. Product groupings - Computers/Electronics/Auto A/C and Mirrors.

10. Management reputation.

11. Serves idle capacity.

12. Fits current capabilities.

*NOTE: The above list is used to select new customers and also to reduce current customer base (we still have customers who do not believe in partnerships).

*Try to develop more nonautomotive customers.

The Magic Workbook, Michigan State University Press, 1999

MAGIC, INC.

27 KEY COMPANIES	4-SLIDE	SMALL STAMP	LARGE STAMP	SPRINGS	ASSEMBLY	PLASTIC	CUSTOMER KNOWLEDGE RELATION-SHIP
BOULDER R&D	$\checkmark*^{2}$	$\checkmark*^{1}$	?	$\checkmark*^{2}$	$\checkmark*^{1}$	$\checkmark*^{1}$	1
LEGENDS R	$\checkmark*^{1}$	$\checkmark*^{1}$	$\checkmark^{1}$	$\checkmark^{?}$	$\checkmark^{1}$	$\checkmark^{1}$	2.0
WARNER R	x	$\checkmark*^{2}$	$\checkmark*^{1}$	x	x	$\checkmark^{?}$	1.5
HERITAGE D	$\checkmark*^{1}$	$\checkmark*^{1}$	$\checkmark*^{1}$	$\checkmark*^{1}$	$\checkmark*^{1}$	$\checkmark*^{1}$	1.5
SHEPHERD D	x	$\checkmark*^{1}$	$\checkmark^{1}$	x	$\checkmark^{1}$	$\checkmark^{1}$	2.5
LAKESIDE R	$\checkmark*^{1}$	$\checkmark*^{1}$	$\checkmark^{1}$	$\checkmark*^{3}$	x	$\checkmark^{1}$	2.4
ATLAS D	$\checkmark*^{1}$	x	x	$\checkmark*^{2}$	$\checkmark^{1}$	$\checkmark^{1}$	1.3
AGS HILLS D	$\checkmark*^{2}$	$\checkmark*^{1}$	$\checkmark^{1}$	$\checkmark*^{2}$	$\checkmark*^{2}$	$\checkmark^{1}$	1.5
GRAYS R&D	$\checkmark*^{?}$	$\checkmark*^{?}$	$\checkmark^{?}$	$\checkmark*^{1}$	$\checkmark*^{1}$	$\checkmark*^{1}$	2
J&M R&D	$\checkmark*^{2}$	$\checkmark*^{1}$	$\checkmark^{1}$	x	$\checkmark*^{1}$	$\checkmark*^{1}$	2
TERRA VALLEY D	$\checkmark*^{1}$	$\checkmark^{?}$	$\checkmark^{1}$	$\checkmark*^{2}$	$\checkmark^{1}$	$\checkmark^{1}$	3
ADVANTAGE D	$\checkmark*^{1}$	$\checkmark^{1}$	$\checkmark^{?}$	$\checkmark*^{1}$	$\checkmark^{1}$	$\checkmark^{1}$	2.5
MASTERSON D	$\checkmark*^{1}$	$\checkmark*^{1}$	$\checkmark^{1}$	$\checkmark*^{2}$	$\checkmark^{1}$	$\checkmark*^{1}$	2
BARNEY R	$\checkmark*^{2}$	$\checkmark*^{?}$	x	$\checkmark*^{1}$	$\checkmark*^{1}$	$\checkmark^{1}$	2
BADGER D	?	$\checkmark*^{1}$	?	?	?*	?	3.0
CREST R	$\checkmark^{3}$	$\checkmark^{1}$	x	$\checkmark*^{1}$	$\checkmark^{?}$	$\checkmark^{?}$	1.5
MILLBROOK D	x^{3}	$\checkmark*^{1}$	$\checkmark^{1}$	x	$\checkmark*^{1}$	$\checkmark^{3}$	2.5
SUNLAKE R	$\checkmark^{?}$	$\checkmark*^{1}$	$\checkmark$	$\checkmark$	$?*^{3}$	$\checkmark$	3
VICTORY D	$\checkmark*^{3}$	$\checkmark*^{1}$	x	$\checkmark*^{1}$	x	x	2
PRESTIGE R	$\checkmark*^{1}$	$\checkmark*^{1}$	$\checkmark^{1}$	$\checkmark^{1}$	$\checkmark^{?}$	$\checkmark^{?}$	2.75
CUSTOM D	$\checkmark*^{1}$	$\checkmark*^{1}$	$\checkmark^{?}$	$\checkmark*^{1}$	$\checkmark*^{1}$	x	2.0
NORTHERN D	$\checkmark*^{1}$	$\checkmark*^{1}$	$\checkmark^{1}$	$\checkmark*^{2}$	$\checkmark*^{?}$	$\checkmark^{1}$	2.0
METAL CITY R&D	$\checkmark*^{2}$	$\checkmark*^{2}$	$\checkmark^{2}$	$\checkmark*^{1}$	$\checkmark*^{1}$	$\checkmark*^{1}$	2.5
SCOTCH D	$\checkmark*^{2}$	$\checkmark*^{2}$	$\checkmark^{1}$	$\checkmark*^{?}$	$\checkmark^{1}$	$\checkmark^{1}$	3
DESKEN D	$\checkmark*^{3}$	$\checkmark*^{1}$	x	$\checkmark*^{2}$	$\checkmark^{3}$	$\checkmark^{3}$	2

LEGEND	
*	Work is currently being done.
✓	Do they buy but not supplier
1	Strong Relationship
2	Some Relationship
3	Weak\unkown
x	No
?	
D	Direct
R	Rep

MAGIC, INC.

GROWTH POTENTIAL	STAMPING/4-SLIDE	SPRINGS
1. LARGE	200,000	50,000
2. MEDIUM	100,000 - 199,000	25,000
3. LIMITED	LESS THAN 100,000	LESS THAN 25,000

^{1} = STRONG RELATIONSHIP
^{2} = SOME RELATIONSHIP
^{3} = WEAK/UNKNOWN

NOTE: These were the sales dollars when we had a larger customer base. Today we are talking millions of sales dollars per customer.

The Magic Workbook, Michigan State University Press, 1999

Magic, Inc.

KEY COMPETITIVE ELEMENTS BY SIC

	CV	EL	GM	GT	MD	MM	OF	SF
Desirable Recession Proof	L	H	L	H	H	M	L	H
Balanced Use of Capacity	L	H	M	H	H	H	H	H
Size of Margin	M/L	H	L	L	L	M	M	M
Competencies	M	H	H	L	M	H	H	H
Weighted Desirability*	5.5	12	7	8	9	10	9	6

CV = Conveyor
EL = Electronics
GM = Gaming

GT = Government
MD = Medical
MM = Miscellaneous Manufacturers

OF = Office Furniture
SF = Store Fixture

H = High (Desirable)   M = Medium   L = Low (Least Desirable)

*H = 3   M = 2   L = 1 - Weighing Methodology

Key elements

ROBUST PROCESS

Quality should become an epidemic in your organization, and everyone should be infected. To achieve our goal of less than ten defective parts produced per million pieces, we use what we refer to as the "Fram Theory." One of Fram oil filters' advertisements claims, "Pay me now or pay me later." The same philosophy holds for us: pay now for the right process or pay later for the mistakes of an incomplete process.

- We have developed a "robust process" that requires every key individual in the process from concept to production to be involved in the planning and the first production run. This requires more time before bringing a new part into actual production, but this well-spent time eliminates worker frustrations, late shipments, and assures quality parts later on. To kill the problems before they begin is our goal. We refine the process as we learn how to do things better. It sounds simple, but in the heat of battle, it's difficult to stick to.
- We sit down with all the key functional players and with a facilitator and list all the steps and problems in the process. Next, we list how we can deliver a part to the factory floor so that when actual production runs there will be no difficulties of any kind. The attached exhibit is our latest version of the steps we go through before putting a new part into production.
- Keeping engineers focused on each part until production signs off on the design and tooling has been a big challenge. Many times because of busy schedules, engineers aren't available for tryouts and first-piece sample submission. Getting the customer to sign off on design changes and providing current blueprints can also be challenging.

The design of a product represents a 70 percent cost impact on the total product cost. This was first established by the automotive companies. More recent studies show that over 90 percent of the final product costs is impacted by the design. It's important to put time and effort into the design—remember, pay me now or pay me later. Our robust process is crucial not only for controlling costs, but also for repeatable quality and the removal of worker dissatisfaction.

Robust Process

The MAGIC Robust Process is a series of meetings and steps developed to provide the necessary communication and interaction between appropriate departments for all new jobs and applicable engineering or process changes. This process provides a standard procedure that will allow all departments involved in producing the product to review the requirements expected by the customer. It provides a standardized means of documenting any concerns or issues through the use of the meeting minutes and checklists indicated in the procedure. It also provides a means of "closing the loop" by verifying that open issues have been resolved by the Sample Submission Run.

The Robust Process is as follows:

I. **New Job Release**

    A. Objective: To provide thorough and accurate information through a standard New Job Release package.

    B. Procedure: 1. Upon notification from the customer, the Sales Department will issue copies of the New Job Go-Ahead (NJGA) to the appropriate departments. Attached to the Engineering copy will be copies of the MAGIC quote to the customer, the MAGIC tooling quote, if applicable, and any additional customer specifications or documents pertinent to the project.

    2. The Engineering Manager will assign a Project Engineer to the project. The Project Engineer will create an Engineering File (hard copy) and place the NJGA in that file.

    3. The Engineering Department will initiate Document Control and Recordkeeping according to **QWI 05.05** (Processing Paperwork upon Receipt of NJGA).

    C. Closing the loop:

1. Within one week of receipt of the NJGA, the Project Engineer will meet with the

Sales Manager for the Pre-launch Meeting to review the customer's requirements.

2. The New Job Go-Ahead will be reviewed at the Project Launch meeting.

D. Forms: 1. MAGIC152 - New Job Go-Ahead

E. Responsible Department: Sales/Engineering

II. Pre-launch Meeting

A. Objective: To review the information provided in the NJGA and list any open issues or

questions. Responsibility for resolution of open issues will be assigned at this time.

B. Procedure: 1. The Project Engineer and the Sales Manager (and/or the responsible Sales

Person) will review the NJGA. All open issues are listed on the Project Launch

Meeting minutes. The person responsible for resolution of the open issue is

assigned. The estimated closing date for the issues is noted.

2. The preliminary Process Flow will be determined and documented on the Process

Flow Chart.

3. The Project Engineer will schedule the project for review at the next Launch

Meeting.

C. Closing the loop:

1. The Project Launch Meeting minutes will be reviewed by the Robust Committee

after the Project Launch Meeting.

2. The Project Launch Meeting minutes will also be reviewed by Department

representatives at the Sample Submission Run.

D. Forms: 1. MAGIC120 - Project Launch Meeting

    2. MAGIC101 - Process Flow Chart

  E. Responsible Department: Sales/Engineering

III. Project Launch Meeting

  A. Objective: To introduce new projects to the departments involved with the manufacture and processing of the product. To clarify the information provided, identify needs for additional information, and discuss areas of concern regarding the manufacture of this product.

  B. Procedure: 1. The Sales Department and the Project Engineer will present to the Launch Meeting attendees a copy of the part drawing, the New Job Go-Ahead, the Process Flowchart, and the Open Issues list from the Pre-launch Meeting.

  2. Any unanswered questions and additional open issues will be added to the Open Issues list on the Project Launch Meeting minutes. The person responsible for addressing each open issue will be assigned at this time. along with an estimated closure date.

  3. Dimensions critical to the customer will be discussed and determined at this meeting. This information will be documented on the Project Launch Meeting Minutes.

  C. Closing the loop:

  1. The Open Issues will be presented to the Robust Committee at the next scheduled Robust Committee meeting.

2. As issues on the Open Issue list are resolved the Project Engineer will indicate the resolution and the date of resolution. This list will be brought to the Sample Submission Run for review by the producing department.

D. Forms: 1. MAGIC120 - Project Launch Meeting

E. Responsible Department: Sales/Engineering

IV. Tooling Design

A. Objective: To review the customer's print and specifications so that tooling can be designed that will allow the manufacture of product to the MAGIC specifications and the customer requirements.

NOTE: This procedure applies to all tooling and all special equipment required for the manufacture of the product. Additional Tooling Design meetings involving the appropriate production personnel will be held and documented.

B. Procedure: 1. The Tooling Supervisor and the Project Engineer will schedule the tooling design meeting for this project. At least one representative of the production department will be present.

2. Along with developing tooling concepts, items to be reviewed and discussed include the customer critical dimensions and the MAGIC processing critical dimensions.

3. Additional questions and open issues from the Tooling Meeting will be noted on the Tooling Meeting Minutes and will be resolved by the Project Engineer and/or Sales Department.

4. Following the Tooling meeting, the Tooling Supervisor(s) will update the Design

of New Tools Report (for fourslide and pressroom tooling) and the Tooling Schedule

(for spring/torsion tooling) with estimated target dates for tool completion milestones.

5. Following the Tooling meeting, a preliminary FMEA will be completed by the Project

Engineer.

C. Closing the loop:

1. A copy of the Tool Design Meeting Minutes is placed in the Engineering file by

the Project Engineer.

2. The Tool Design Meeting Minutes will be reviewed by the production department at

the Sample Submission Run for closure of all open issues.

3. The final tooling design will be reviewed and approved by the Tooling Supervisor,

the Project Engineer, and a representative of the production department.

4. Following completion of the tooling design, the Project Engineer will report the

material requirements (stock width and progression) to the Sales Department. The

Sales Department will issue a notification to the appropriate departments so that tryout

material is ordered. This step is not applicable for spring/torsion tooling.

D. Forms: 1. MAGIC107 - Tool Design Meeting Minutes
2. Design of New Tools Report - Path: G:\Toolroom\Wade\Newtools.xls
3. Tooling Schedule - Path: G:\Fpw26\Schedule\Start.prg
4. MAGIC102 - FMEA (Failure Mode and Effects Analysis)

E. Responsible Department: Engineering/Tooling

V. Quality Planning Meeting

A. Objective: To review critical dimensions and determine necessary gages and/or techniques for measurement. To finalize the Control Plan

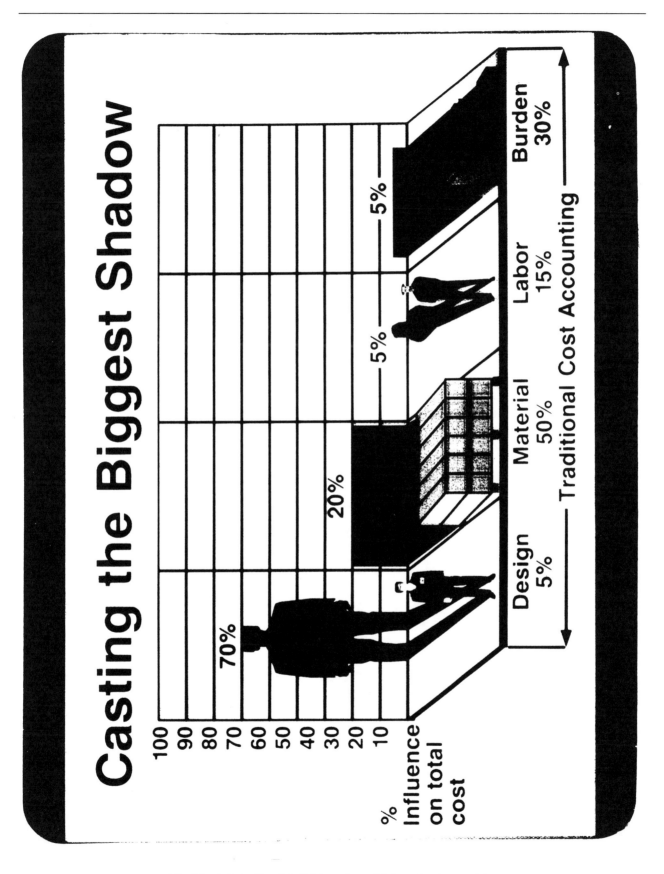

Casting the Biggest Shadow

COST COMMITMENT CURVE

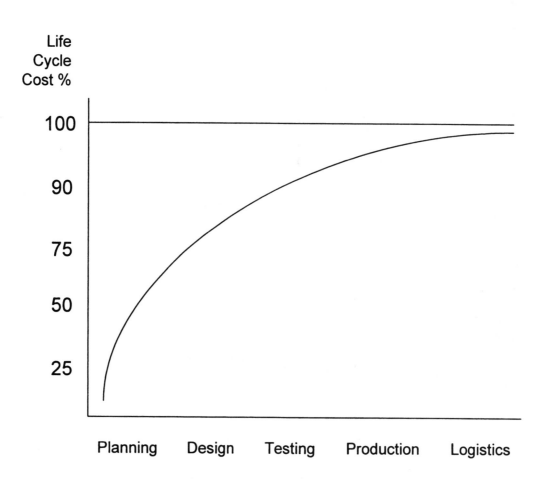

By the end of the development stage, at least
90 percent of the left-cycle costs are *committed
by not incurred.*

The Magic Workbook, Michigan State University Press, 1999

VISION

Vision is the ability to see where you are going. A captain of a ship has a vision for how to get to his destination. The captain has a plan and an internal view of what it will be like when the ship arrives. As Proverbs says, "Without a vision, the people perish." Of course the captain must convey this vision to the crew, and the crew must catch and believe in the captain's passion. After all, the captain cannot sail the ship by himself. Then, together, the captain and crew must hew to their vision of the future. So it is with organizations. Too many owners manage by the seat of their pants and change course with every crisis. Action without vision is a nightmare. Vision without action is a daydream.

Effective vision statements briefly and succinctly address measurement and operations as well as what will revolutionize an industry. The classic example of this is Federal Express's vision statement: "We will deliver by 10:30 the next morning." Federal Express revolutionized the movement of packages. The message was clear, crisp, and understood by all.

Once a vision is created, it cannot become reality unless it is managed into reality. When formulating a vision, do not dwell on the corporate beatitudes. Such feel-good statements have little impact on day-to-day decisions. There is a fine line between a vision and hallucination.

Many companies confuse a mission statement with a vision statement. A vision statement is where you are headed; the mission statement is how you are planning to get there. Another key component in a corporate constitution is a value statement, the philosophy by which the organization deals with its employees, customers, suppliers, stakeholders, and community. All three provide leadership to the organization.

- The cyclists exhibit illustrates that we are always peddling to a distant vision. The path never ends. The bicycle sprocket stands for the "Plan, Do, Act, and Check" (PDCA) cycle that Ed Deming made well known. The wheels represent the SDCA cycle of Standardize, Do, Check, and Act. We are continually turning the sprocket and wheels to achieve quality and drive toward our distant vision. Another exhibit illustrates our belief that without standardizing we move very slowly, if at all, toward our vision.

- Our associates annually revisit our vision at one of our lifelong education sessions to review our statements—along with an action plan—and to suggest any changes that they feel are beneficial and necessary. Everyone is asked to sign the statement after we discuss suggested changes and make the appropriate ones. These statements are then posted on the many information boards located throughout our plant.

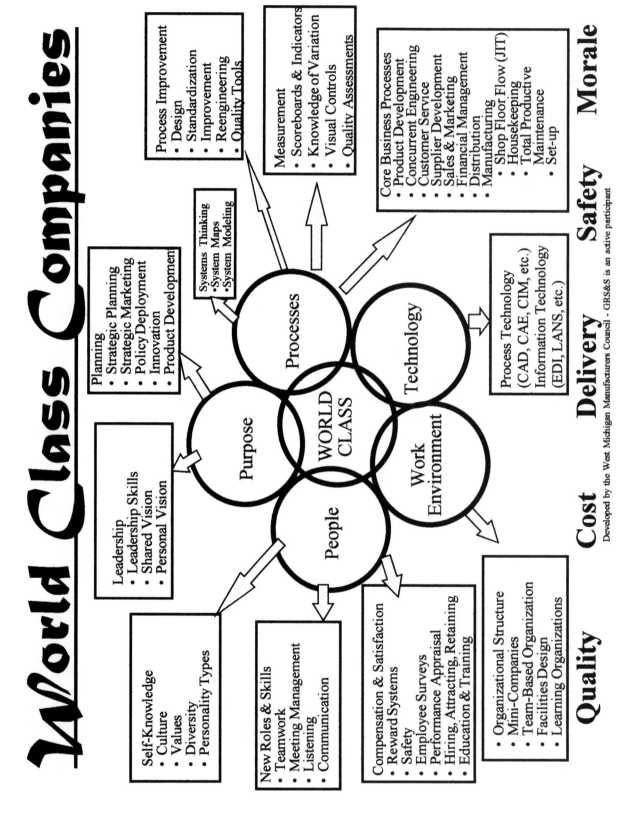

World Class Companies

Planning
- Strategic Planning
- Strategic Marketing
- Policy Deployment
- Innovation
- Product Development

Systems Thinking
- System Maps
- System Modeling

Process Improvement
- Design
- Standardization
- Improvement
- Reengineering
- Quality Tools

Measurement
- Scoreboards & Indicators
- Knowledge of Variation
- Visual Controls
- Quality Assessments

Core Business Processes
- Product Development
- Concurrent Engineering
- Customer Service
- Supplier Development
- Sales & Marketing
- Financial Management
- Distribution
- Manufacturing
  - Shop Floor Flow (JIT)
  - Housekeeping
  - Total Productive Maintenance
  - Set-up

Leadership
- Leadership Skills
- Shared Vision
- Personal Vision

Self-Knowledge
- Culture
- Values
- Diversity
- Personality Types

New Roles & Skills
- Teamwork
- Meeting Management
- Listening
- Communication

Compensation & Satisfaction
- Reward Systems
- Safety
- Employee Surveys
- Performance Appraisal
- Hiring, Attracting, Retaining
- Education & Training

- Organizational Structure
- Mini-Companies
- Team-Based Organization
- Facilities Design
- Learning Organizations

Process Technology
(CAD, CAE, CIM, etc.)
Information Technology
(EDI, LANS, etc.)

Circles: Processes, Purpose, WORLD CLASS, Technology, Work Environment, People

Quality   Cost   Delivery   Safety   Morale

Developed by the West Michigan Manufacturers Council - GRS&S is an active participant

The Magic Workbook, Michigan State University Press, 1999

PURPOSE
(Doing the Right Things)

1. What customers/markets do I want to pursue?
2. Strategic direction and intent (business vision/mission)
3. Collecting the voice of customer information

PURPOSE

PROCESSES (TQM)

1. QCDSM Scoreboards (that measure/report variation; use SPC)
2. Systems documentation (flow charts)
3. Making decisions and solving complex problems (based on data used in the seven step PDCA process: Process improvement teams: suggestion system)

PROCESSES (TQM)

PEOPLE

1. Tapping into the capabilities of people through learning organizations (aspiration, conversation, complexity)
2. Transformation of culture through empowerment and teamwork.
3. Organizational development

PEOPLE

SYSTEMS

PEOPLE

| PDCA | CUSTOMERS | VARIATION |
| PLANNED CHANGE | **TQM PRINCIPLES** | VISUAL COMMUNICATION |

Developed by the West Michigan Manufacturers Council - GRS&S is an active participant

VISION

Corporate vision determines where an organization hopes to go and how it intends to get there.

Grounded in both intuition and purpose, a well-defined vision challenges members of an organization to work together in pursuing lofty but practical goals.

Vision -- a common theme to inform all workers of the company's changes and restructurings.

Visionary organizations anticipate change and identify opportunities.

Many companies define or redefine vision when external challenges threaten operations.

By acting boldly when changing patterns become clear, companies gain wide latitude for their actions and set precedents for others to follow.

Any number of problems, like unforeseen events or poor planning or implementation, can impede a vision.

The Magic Workbook, Michigan State University Press, 1999

Mission Statement

You should bear in mind the following questions in assessing your statement and in rewriting it or in writing a mission statement from scratch.

Questions for Self-Examination

1. Does the statement reinforce the organization as something one should identify with and which deserves admiration from employees, customers, vendors, stockholders, and the community?

2. Does it provide a rallying point, uniting people so they feel satisfaction in working toward a common goal?

3. Does the mission statement focus on quality, continuous improvement, and customer satisfaction?

4. Does it stress the needs of employees with respect to their long-term value to the company as a critical resource?

5. Does the statement take a long-term view, committing the company to developing new products and services for the future, and putting resources into training, research, and education?

6. Does it take into account all those concerned with the company's ultimate survival, such as vendors, customers, stockholders, and employees?

7. Will company purposes, as established in the mission statement, remain constant despite changes in top management?

The above questions should help you organize your thinking about your firm's mission statement.

Mission

Provide high-quality, competitively priced voice, data, video, and wireless communications services that enhance our customers' work, learning, and leisure. Lead our markets in customer satisfaction and loyalty. Foster employee commitment, initiative, and effectiveness. Increase the value of our shareowners' investment.

Pacific Telesis

VALUES

Six shared values guide all our efforts in a diverse and changing marketplace:

- •We focus on the customer.

- •We value the individual—and reward teamwork.

- •We encourage clear, open communication.

- •We strive to be the best at what we do.

- •We prize creative, can-do people.

- •We deliver on the bottom line—for customers and shareowners.

Pacific Telesis

(170 associate signitures not reprinted —security reasons)

MAGIC, INC.

138 ERIE ST, CHICAGO IL 60671 • (630) 555-4491 fax (630) 555-0951

October 1998

VISION AND MISSION STATEMENT

VISION: "BEST AT WHAT WE DO"

To be recognized by our stakeholders (customers, associates, suppliers, and stockholders) as a leader in the manufacturing of stampings, springs, slide formed parts and value added assemblies.

"WITHOUT A VISION THE PEOPLE PERISH"
Proverbs 29:18

MISSION: "PROFITS THROUGH QUALITY AND HAVE FUN DURING THE PROCESS"

Grow our associates and build high-trust relationships with stakeholders; leading an empowered and involved workforce through T.R.I.C. and use our Mini-Company concepts as performance measurements.

ACTION PLAN: Continuous development of our associates' potential. This will be accomplished by an informed, stable, and skilled workforce through:

a) Focus on customer needs - using Quality, Cost, Delivery, Safety, and Morale as our drivers.

b) ISO/QS Maintain Registration - Continued implementation for improvement (Continuous Improvement, Constancy of Purpose).

c) Training and Education programs to develop leadership and technological excellence.

d) Tools for Good Time Management.

e) Adherence to and refinement of our Robust Process.

f) Technology - Exposure to the latest capabilities; develop and adopt where appropriate.

g) Pay for performance based on contributions to MAGIC

h) Celebrations and recognition for successes.

i) Continued re-enforcement of T.R.I.C. (Trust, Relationship, Integrity, Communications).

"THE ROAD TO THE FUTURE"

Developed by Florida Power & Light while working with Dr. Deming for The Deming Award

STEPS TO THE FUTURE

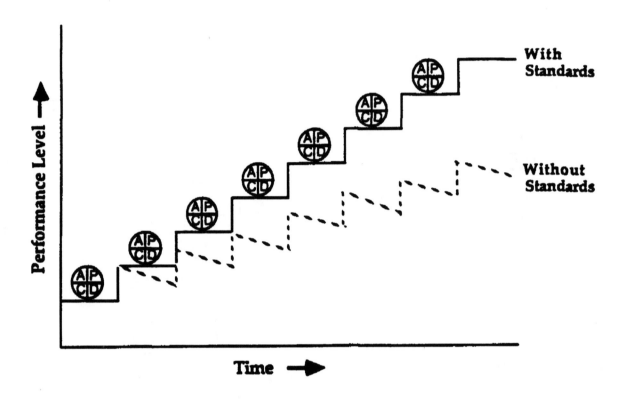

P = PLAN
D = DO
C = CHECK
A = ACT

The Magic Workbook, Michigan State University Press, 1999

MAGIC, INC
CONTINUOUS IMPROVEMENT STORY

THEME:

BACKGROUND / TEAM INFO (P C) (PLAN)	1) DEFINE THE CURRENT SITUATION / SYSTEM (P C) (PLAN)
2) CURRENT SITUATION (P C) (PLAN)	3) ANALYZE CAUSES (P C) (PLAN)
4) TRY OUT IMPROVEMENT / SOLUTIONS (P C) (DO)	5) STUDY THE RESULTS (P C) (CHECK)
6) STANDARDIZATION (P C) (ACT)	7) PLAN NEXT IMPROVEMENT (P C) (ACT)

8) PRESENTATION/CELEBRATE!

COMMUNICATIONS

This is probably the most overused suggestion for improving a company. You can never have too much communication, yet everyone cannot be involved in every decision. We think that our associates are in meetings or learning experiences about 1 1/2 hours per week. Is that enough? When we do our annual associate survey, the area mentioned the most for improvement is communications, both from the top down and from the floor to the president without going through many layers of management. We do not believe you should have to go through different levels to speak to an associate.

We started by having weekly departmental meetings. The lead (we do not use the term supervisor) of the department holds the meeting. Problem experienced:

- Not every lead thought it was important to have a weekly meeting. Many from the old school thought, "I am the boss, they do not need to know. Do what I say."
- Many of the leads did not know how to hold a meeting or were afraid to stand in front of a group and talk.

Several things had to happen. Some leads had to leave because they could not abandon the old style of management. Others had to learn how to communicate effectively. Of course, when we talk about the importance of culture, it starts with management.

Tools we are currently using to communicate:

- Departmental huddles before each shift for each department.
- We are now organized into Mini-Companies, which are cross-functional, self-directed work teams.
- We meet once a week as a mini-company with all associates for 45 to 60 minutes. Focus on QCDSM, review progress, and if there is a problem, form a team to do problem solving and report back at future meetings.
- Management of the mini-company holds its own preparation meetings before the company weekly meetings.
- All mini-company officers meet once a week to compare notes about improvements.
- Mini-company officers meet once a month with the company's internal bankers—the president and two vice-presidents—to present reports tracking monthly and annual QCDSM.
- Twice a year we have a trade show where the mini-companies share with the whole plant the improvements made in the last six months. We move from department to department so that we can actually see the improvements. **This is a form of internal networking.**
- There are at least three mini-company officers: manufacturing, quality, and technical.

- A TV monitor system throughout the plant lists birthdays and anniversaries, visitors, vision and mission statements, and meeting schedules for various committees.
- Bulletin boards and visual communication throughout the plant show customer quality ratings, company delivery performance, and inventory levels.
- A KPI board in the cafe shows month and year-to-date on all that we measure and track—cost of quality, parts per million defects, customer concerns, CPK, customer returns, profitability, sales to payroll dollars, inventory, weekly delivery performance, accidents and accidents that require outside medical attention, implemented ideas, tardiness and absences, and housekeeping or workplace organization.

HOW IS THE COMPANY POLICY SHARED WITHIN THE ORGANIZATION?

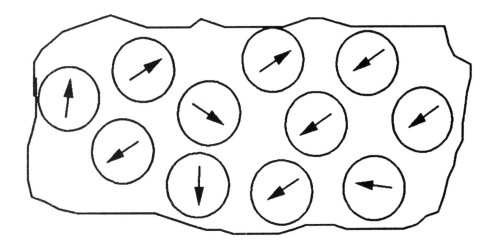

IS IT LIKE THIS?

OR ... LIKE THIS?

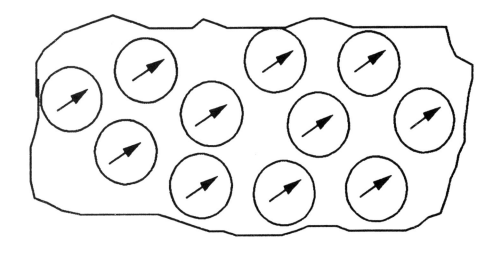

The Magic Workbook, Michigan State University Press, 1999

Reprinted with permission from *The New Shop Floor Management* by Kio Suzaki.

CULTURE FOCUS GROUP

PURPOSE: Development through 'Herbie' (constraint) identification. Meeting to continue team work, cooperation, communication, trust, positive thinking, and calling for "Betterment not Bitterment" among all departments and shifts. Each associate takes responsibility for the quality of his or her work and for helping others where necessary. Separate committees for each building.

CHAIR-PERSON: President

MEMBERS: Six active members

MINI - CO   MEETINGS

PURPOSE: To provide a method for distribution of information to company associates.

CHAIR - PERSON: Mini - Co. Officer (3 officers from each Mini-Co.).

MEMBERS: Member of the Mini-Co. and either the General Manager, Plant Manager, Quality Manager, or Engineering Manager.

WORKPLACE ORGANIZATION

PURPOSE: To set standards and do weekly inspection to compare each department to a standard. Monthly celebrations for most improved.

CO-CHAIR-PERSONS: Plant Personnel

MEMBERS: Eight associates who come to monthly meetings; each member inspects complete plant individually.

MINI - CO OFFICER MEETINGS

PURPOSE: To provide a timely and consistent method for distribution of information and review and implementation of the mini-company business plan.

CHAIR-PERSON: Mini-company

MEMBERS: Officers of the Mini-Co.

MATERIAL REVIEW BOARD (MRB)

PURPOSE: To assure timely, cost-effective, and acceptable disposition of material rejected as defective product or suspected of being defective.

CHAIR-PERSON: General Manager/VP

MEMBERS: General Manager, Plant Manger, Quality Manager, Materials Manager, and Customer Service, Quality Resource Representative as required.

PREVENTIVE MAINTENANCE

PURPOSE: To review procedures and set standards for preventive maintenance for the complete plant and all the equipment.

CHAIR-PERSON: Maintenance Lead

MEMBERS: Plant Personnel from departments. Meet monthly.

| Fourslide | Shipping/Receiving | Tool Room | Maintenance |
| Press Room | Value Added - PR | Value Added - FS | Spring |

PRODUCTION PLANNING MEETING

PURPOSE: To prioritize and consistently communicate weekly production schedules and any difficulties.
CHAIR-PERSON: Production Coordinator

MEMBERS: Customer Service Representative, Production Coordinator.   Separate meetings for each

production department discipline. Department Leads as required.

SAFETY COMMITTEE MEETING

PURPOSE: To set policies that deal with safety. To review all accidents and incidents. To act as an
advisory board for discipline of any of the policies.
CHAIR-PERSON: Engineering Manager

MEMBERS: Mini-co. representatives. First Thursday of every month.

SAMPLE BOARD

PURPOSE: To provide a visual reference with approved standards for use by Manufacturing, Shipping,
and Quality Assurance personnel.
CHAIR-PERSON: Plant Manager

MEMBERS: Associates representing Shipping/Receiving, Quality Assurance, Fourslide, Secondary, Spring
Torsion, and Press Room and Engineering.

DESCRIPTION: The ultimate goal of this group is to provide a visual aid for any purpose
(identification, plating, set-up, etc.). It is not to be used for critical dimensions.
The group meets on a monthly basis and has reached a 95% + completion
success. The Sample Board also serves as a sales tool to show existing and
potential new customers our wide range of products.
The Sample Board also gives departments a sense of ownership. Each
lead is proud to not only use their Board as they see fit, but it also serves
as a topic of discussion during a lead departmental plant tour.

ROBUST

PURPOSE: To provide a forum for review of feasibility, capability, and customer requirements
associated with new tools. Also, to discuss & solve ongoing Quality/Mfg. concerns.
CHAIR-PERSON: General Manager/VP & Engineering Manager

MEMBERS: General Manager/VP, Plant Manager, Engineering CQE, Engineering Manger,

Material Manager, Spring Engineer, QA Manager, and Sales Manager.

STAFF MEETINGS

PURPOSE: To provide a timely and consistent method for distribution of information throughout
the company.
CHAIR-PERSON: President

MEMBERS: President, General Manager/VP, Plant Manager, Quality Assurance Manager,
Administrative Manager, Sales Manager, Tooling/Engineering Manager, Controller.

STRATEGIC PRODUCTION PLANNING

PURPOSE: To recognize and coordinate resources to meet future requirements (Man, Materials, Methods, etc.).

CHAIR-PERSON: Plant Manager

MEMBERS: Sales Manager, Production Coordinator, Accounting Manager, Materials Manager.

FOURSILDE SET-UP REDUCTION CIUG

PURPOSE: To standardize tooling and processing as it relates to the reduction of set-up time of Fourslide machines.

CHAIR-PERSON: Plant Manager

MEMBERS: Fourslide Production Lead, Fourslide toolmaker, Fourslide set-up person (in conjunction with seven outside companies).

SKILLS CHARTING FOCUS GROUP

PURPOSE: To coordinate and standardize the various skills charting activities within the plant. To help implement effective training as it relates to QA, technical skills, and preventive maintenance.

CHAIR-PERSON: Plant Manager

MEMBERS: QA Resource Press Room/Fourslide, Material Manager, QA Resource Secondary, QA Resource Spring, Training Director.

PLANNING "ARE YOU READY GROUP"

PURPOSE: To effectively implement various projects within the plant. To effectively communicate to the various disciplines to avoid duplication of efforts.

CHAIR-PERSON: General Manager/VP

MEMBERS: Plant Manager, Engineering Manager, Sales Manager, Electronics Technician, Toolroom Supervisor, Prototype Lead, and President.

"BANKERS MEETING"

PURPOSE: To provide a system to review, encourage, and assist the Mini - Company officers in the implementation of the business plan as it relates to Q.C.D.S. & M.

CHAIR-PERSON: President, Plant Manager, General Manager/VP

MEMBERS: All mini-co. officers

The Magic Workbook, Michigan State University Press, 1999

CULTURE

Positive culture is like esprit de corps: You can sense it, but it is difficult to articulate or measure. We recognized from the beginning that without a healthy culture at Magic, changes would be difficult to achieve and maintain over time. Autocratic dictates do not allow individuals to take ownership of their company.

Culture is also like gravity—a very powerful, yet invisible force pulling people in a certain direction. Unfortunately, many organizations don't recognize the impact of culture on behavior. By failing to clearly define and communicate culture, organizations leave themselves open to all kinds of misunderstandings and conflicts.

Every organization has a culture by default. Many organizations only allow it to happen, but management must work overtime to build a culture of trust and relationships. That kind of culture won't happen by default. You have to spend time together to build relationships. In the beginning, we did this by having monthly meetings with the leads and discussing various issues, problems, and plans. After the meetings we all went to the local pizza place for food and libations and to continue talking about whatever. This started to build understanding, friendships, and trust. The company also purchased new tools, equipment, and other items requested by the associates—another concrete sign that management was going to walk its talk about concern for associates.

- We hold companywide, departmental, and lead meetings where our plans, expectations, and goals are shared. Feedback and dialogue are encouraged. We spend time talking about the "whys" behind our actions—why housekeeping and safety are so important, for example.
- A cross-functional culture committee meets once a month to discuss possible cultural events and how to improve relationships between and among associates. Minutes are posted on information boards. One of the goals of the committee is to involve as many people as possible in our cultural events.
- Each year we have cultural events around Patriots Day; best Halloween costume; best Halloween pumpkin; Crazy Hat Day; Crazy T-shirt Day; Christmas and Thanksgiving dinners; an annual picnic with clowns and children's rides and games; annual bowling, fishing, and golf outings; many shared lunches where everyone brings a dish to pass; tickets to local professional basketball, hockey, and baseball teams; fund-raisers for charitable associations; an annual barbecue cooked by management for all employees; an annual spring clean-up day; and so on. We have an event on average every two weeks.

"Quality People Make Quality Products"

MAGIC, INC.

The Magic Workbook, Michigan State University Press, 1999

HAPPY HOLIDAYS 1998

The Associates of MAGIC would like to wish you and your families the best for the holiday season and thank you for your support.

*(170 associate signitures
not reprinted — security reasons)*

Springing to World-Class Manufacturing

Grand Rapids Spring & Wire Co. created a culture based on trust and commitment between management and employees.

BY HARPER A. ROEHM,
DONALD J. KLEIN, CMA, AND
JOSEPH F. CASTELLANO

Perhaps the most important components needed for world-class manufacturing (WCM) to succeed are employee involvement and trust. Not only must employees believe in and understand WCM concepts, but they must believe in management's commitment to the changes required. Problems inevitably will arise in the process of converting from a traditional manufacturing model to WCM. That is why in order to create the physical plant and psychological changes required for WCM to occur, the company culture must change. To facilitate the physical, psychological, and cultural changes, management must build trust between it and the employees.

The story of Grand Rapids Spring & Wire Co. (GRSW) illustrates how a small traditional manufacturing firm created the culture and trust with its employees necessary for its successful conversion to a world-class manufacturing environment and operation.

Grand Rapids Spring & Wire Co. was established in 1960 in Grand Rapids, Mich., and purchased by Tim Homan and Jim Zawacki, active partner and president, in June 1985. The company manufactures a variety of products which include compression, extension, and torsion springs; stampings for progressive dies and four-slide products; roll forming; wire and grommet molding; and various assembly processes. Approximately 60% of sales are to automotive companies with the other 40% going to the appliance, furniture, and hardware industries. Total sales for 1989 were approximately $12 million with most of the customers located in the Midwest.

There are more than 1,000 spring companies in the United States and Canada with a total sales market of around $2 billion. Most spring manufacturers operate in specific regions.

Mike Mancewicz, near right, shows off his new numerical control spring machine at GRSW.

The largest spring manufacturing company represents less than 10% of the market. In western Michigan GRSW has six competitors who for the most part have different equipment and, as a result, different capabilities. Sales of its competitors range from $1 million to $18 million, and they employ from eight to 200 people.

Jim Zawacki, president, prefers to call foremen "leads" because this term more closely describes the expectations of the individuals given responsibility for orchestrating the actions of the employees. There are 125 employees at GRSW.

GETTING STARTED

When Jim Zawacki acquired the company in 1985, he was aware that because of competitive pressures, GRSW would need to improve quality and reduce costs. Having worked previously as president of a larger company that spent four years attempting to implement statistical process control, he was convinced that its implementation at GRSW was the essential first step in its goal to improve quality. A statistical process control coordinator was hired to prepare training materials, and several in-house seminars were conducted so that employees would be able to perform SPC manually. Some of the early results were exciting. In the past when problems arose, plant employees' first reaction would be to attempt to adjust their equipment. Now they realized that in many instances the problem was caused by a new reel of wire and possibly the supplier of the wire might be the cause.

In the early stages of trying to improve quality, Jim Zawacki was not aware of all of the elements in a world-class manufacturing environment. In 1986 he was invited by a customer to attend a seminar regarding Richard J. Schonberger's book, *Japanese Manufacturing Techniques: Nine Hidden Lessons In Simplicity.* At the heart of Schonberger's book are two overlapping strategies of "just-in-time" production and "total quality control." Following this meeting, a four-hour session was held with employees in order to explain the basic concepts of world-class manufacturing and why management thought it was necessary for GRSW. The customer, who had invited the owner to the seminar, loaned GRSW audio/videotapes so that each department could view the tapes as a group and attempt to implement the WCM philosophy.

These efforts were not without some frustrations. One of the early attempts to implement suggestions from viewing Schonberger's tapes involved each department placing an easel board in its work area. As employees were confronted with problems, they were asked to record the problem on the easel. Each week the department met as a group and attempted to solve the problems listed. While many sound suggestions were offered, for the most part few changes were implemented. As management later noted, there was fall-through rather than follow-through.

Management also learned that it had not trained employees how to solve problems. It failed in the attempt to implement a technique called single minute exchange of dies because of inadequate training. From September 1986 through June 1987, departments met on a regular basis, viewed approximately one-half of the Schonberger tapes, and were generally unsuccessful in their efforts to bring a WCM philosophy to GRSW.

MOVING FORWARD

In June 1987, an observer was invited to attend the management meetings and view the tapes with the management team. After several months of meetings, management decided to hire the observer as a facilitator with the specific purpose of providing leadership and direction. As the facilitator's first step, each employee was asked to read Eliyahu M. Goldratt's book *The Goal. The Goal* is the story of how a manufacturing plant turned around its performance when it was finally able to identify the real "goal" and the means to achieve it. After several sessions to explain how the concepts in the book

related to GRSW, the facilitator began holding "Herbie" meetings with the employees. ("Herbie" was identified in *The Goal* as a short stocky boy scout who was the constraint on a hike.)

GRSW "Herbie" meetings were designed to identify what employees thought were the root problems (contraints) of GRSW. A constraint is anything that prevents an organization from reaching a higher level of performance as measured against its goal of making more money now and in the future. All of the employees' suggestions elicited from the group sessions were recorded. Many constructive suggestions identified by the employees turned out not to be root causes but symptoms of the real problem. Therefore, the facilitator required each group to focus on root causes instead of symptoms through the effect-cause-effect approach.

Following extensive discussions, each group ranked its "Herbies." The top two "Herbies" from each group were summarized and presented to management, and five major opportunities called the "four + one program" were developed. The management and the employees formulated simple working solutions regarding the five focused problems. Before the facilitator started working on the project, each department identified separate problems and attempted to solve the problems on a weekly and monthly basis. Now the entire plant was focused on five major issues with no definite time commitment for accomplishment.

"If you focus on everything, you focus on nothing," Plato is reported to have said. This lack of focus was one of GRSW's major problems. The "four + one program" provided the needed focus and made it easier for GRSW to communicate with its employees regarding the changes that would have to be made.

Management and the facilitator reviewed all the suggestions that the employees had identified in their brainstorming sessions. The facilitator provided management with a list of all the suggestions by group. In response to some of the employees' suggestions, management determined that the communication process needed to be improved. As a result, managers met with each group in order to discuss and review suggestions. Employees became convinced that management was serious about the "Herbie" process.

MAJOR CONSTRAINT

The need for training and education regarding setup times in the Press Room and Four-

Slide Department was considered to be the major constraint for the entire plant. Most setup times were too long and frequently not performed correctly, thereby causing bad parts to be produced. A series of employee and management meetings diagnosed the cause of the problem: poor tooling and inadequate training.

As a result, management developed the following programs:

- 30-hour seminar to train 50 employees on blueprint reading,
- 16-hour tooling seminar for 25 employees,
- purchase of a videotape series on setup procedures for the Press Room Department.

A tooling expert was hired, and for much of the equipment new tooling was either made or purchased. The results of these efforts caused dramatic reductions in setup times. Many of the press room setups went from an average of four hours to 20 minutes. In the Four-Slide Department the average setup was reduced immediately from an average of eight hours down to under three hours. Not only has reduced setup time increased plant capacity, but it also has reduced its cycle time. These innovations enabled GRSW to gain a competitive advantage through its shorter cycle times and the improved product quality because of its better setup performance.

A second and obvious change needed was better housekeeping. Clutter and general messiness were getting in the way of producing a quality product on a timely basis. Often tools could not be found, it was difficult to walk in aisles, and machinery was not cleaned after being used. Many believed that the plant's appearance contributed in a negative way to the employees' work attitude. Again, employee and management meetings were held and an agreement reached that housekeeping should be everyone's responsibility. Today the plant would pass a white glove inspection.

Management identified the quality of material used in production as the third major problem. In the "Herbie" meetings, employees indicated that there were major problems caused by material where the material was not reported as the problem. For example, when manufacturing a particular spring, plant workers might discover halfway through a spool of wire that the wire was defective. Most of the time the spool would be discarded and a new spool would be ordered without reporting the incident to management. When employees were asked why management usually would not be informed, they replied that when they did tell management rarely was there any follow-up.

At the suggestion of employees, a new procedure was developed for tracking material failures. When a material failure does occur, the employee is instructed to stop the machine immediately and complete an In Process Material Problem (IPMP) form indicating the nature of the problem and request the purchasing manager to review the situation. The purchasing manager then contacts the responsible vendor and provides a written response to the employee's IPMP within 48 hours. Records are maintained on vendor performances and reviewed with the vendors. Based on an analysis of vendor performance, the company has been able to reduce the number of major suppliers from 40 to 20 and in addition receive vendor certification as to the chemical makeup and tensile strength of the wire.

PREVENTIVE MAINTENANCE

Two types of maintenance problems surfaced. First, repairs were not being completed on a timely basis, and, second, many of the required repairs could have been avoided if preventive maintenance had been performed. With employee assistance, both repair and preventive maintenance programs were developed. Any machine that is judged by the worker and lead to need repair is red-tagged. A form developed by employees and management provides space for both a diagram and explanation of the problem. A copy of the form is sent to the plant supervisor who records on a master list the date the problem was identified along with the machine number. The supervisor must schedule the repair within 30 days. Each week at the leads' meeting, the master list of repairs is reviewed to confirm that the red-tagged machine has been included on the master list and that the supervisor has scheduled the repair. Once the repair is completed, the red tag is removed from the machine.

In order to reduce downtime caused by the need for repairs, employees and management established a preventive maintenance program that assigned individuals to specific machines. As preventive maintenance is performed, these individuals must initial a form indicating its completion. Maintenance tools and repair manuals are provided for each machine, and a computer printout summarizes the cost of maintenance. The results of their efforts have substantially reduced machine downtime due to repairs.

SAMPLE BOARDS

The last "Herbie" identified was caused by employees not being certain which parts had to be painted, platted, or heat treated. This uncertainty resulted in shipping parts that did not meet the customer's requirements. To solve this problem, sample boards were built that displayed each part. Prior to shipping or to machine setup, employees visually could verify general appearance of the part. In addition, a certification process developed by the quality assurance department ensured that each sample part was approved prior to being placed on the sample boards. Once the quality assurance personnel were satisfied that the sample part was in conformance with the customer's requirements, the part was painted green, and a tag was prepared with the part number, date, and customer name. This board also has become a useful marketing tool for potential customers visiting the plant. Every six months a designated employee in each department audits the sample board against a computer printout as to what should be on the board.

STRENGTHENING TRUST

For each of the four + one opportunities, employees and management worked together as a team in identifying the constraint, in diagnosing its cause, and in recommending a simple solution. In addition, management followed through by providing the necessary resources both in time and dollars in order to achieve a satisfactory resolution of each problem. As employees

began to participate in a meaningful way, trust began to grow. Other elements in the process of converting to WCM also strengthened employee trust.

From the initial commitment by Jim Zawacki to move toward a WCM environment until the present, management has attempted to communicate fully with employees as well as listen to their suggestions. Employees' ideas have been used in solving problems. The management of GRSW demonstrated its commitment to world-class management and to employees as the four + one program moved forward.

Within general guidelines, Jim Zawacki allowed an employee committee to determine merit pay increases for all employees. A representative committee was established in which individual performances were reviewed and recommendations made to management. Furthermore a bonus system based on quality improvements and profits was established. Under the plan a base period was established with labor as a percentage of sales (after sales had been adjusted for rejects and returned sales). To the extent that employees were able in a future time period to reduce this percentage as compared to the base period, they were allowed to share in the savings in the form of bonuses. Employees interviewed for this article stated that they became true believers in WCM *after* receiving their first bonus check.

In addition to striving to improve communications, to listening, to adopting employee suggestions, and to allowing workers to share in improvements in quality, management has attempted to respond to other employee needs not normally considered management's responsibility. The company's training efforts also have

Employees brainstorm improvements at one of GRSW's "Herbie" sessions.

The Magic Workbook, Michigan State University Press, 1999

indicated to labor management's confidence in them and the seriousness of their commitment to WCM. Throughout the process a great deal of time and money has been devoted to employee training.

In addition to the many programs already mentioned, the firm provides a tuition rebate and an apprenticeship program for tool and die making and four-slide setup. A film library has been established where employees can earn incentives for reviewing certain tapes. They also have invested in a plantwide computerized statistical process control system using electronic measuring instruments. Employees and their spouses were provided the opportunity at GRSW's expense to participate in weight loss, no smoking, and nutrition programs, as well as CPR and first aid training.

These initiatives have paid large dividends to GRSW. Recently the individual who was responsible for heat treating spring products left the company. As the firm prepared to replace him another employee suggested that a portable oven could be moved next to the spring machine and that with a minor adjustment springs could be automatically transported to and through the heat treating oven. The suggestion was adopted and, as a result, it was not necessary to replace the employee. In addition, the innovation added to available plant space. Employees also have played a significant role in rearranging other equipment throughout the plant.

Attitudes have changed significantly. In the past, employees would be waiting at 2:45 p.m. to clock out at 3:00 p.m. Now they do not have to be asked to stay longer if it is required to complete a job. Past-dues have improved from 60% on-time shipments to 97% on-time. Cost of quality has improved from 6% to 2.7% of sales, and parts defective per million (PPM) has registered a 1,000% improvement. Perhaps the most significant achievement has been the company's product acceptance by Japanese firms and the continuous development of more working relationships with world-class manufacturers.

The four + one program was initiated in January 1989, and by September everyone in the company sensed the changes in attitudes and the emergence of a new culture. The four + one program had instilled pride and a sense of ownership. At the present time GRSW is working on Total Quality Management. The committees for the four + one program continue to meet once a month to review their progress and search for areas of improvement.

Finally, GRSW has increased sales more than 50% and profits by an even greater percentage, while inventories have decreased by more than 30%.

ACCOUNTING MEASUREMENTS

At the outset a decision was made by management not to be concerned about the effects the proposed changes would have on the firm's accounting system. Although Jim Zawacki was a trained accountant and had worked as a management accountant, he was content to rely essentially on cash flow analysis as the primary tool for decision making.

In addition, management believed that it had an intuitive sense as to the cost data (i.e., direct materials and labor) needed for competitive bidding purposes. Consequently, very little consideration was given to developing a traditional standard for direct costing system. GRSW did adopt *The Goal's* financial concepts of Throughput (T), Operating Expenses (OE), and Inventory/Investment (I). Throughput is the rate at which the system generates dollars through sales, operating expenses are the funds the system invests in purchasing what it intends to sell, and investment is the money the system spends in turning inventory into Throughput. In other words, cash is either coming in (T), going out (OE), or staying within GRSW (I).

All employees are required to ask themselves what effects their actions and decisions have on T, OE, and I. Indirectly, the employee's favorable action on one or all of these financial measurements automatically impacts on the macro financial measurements of net profit and return on investment.

The use of these micro financial measurements of T, OE, and I tie back to the macro measurements.

All employees at GRSW understand these measurements and how favorably or unfavorably their decisions will impact the measurements. This accounting system has been very successful at GRSW. Even with a slowing of the economy, GRSW continues to show month-to-month higher sales and net profit. Any additional changes in the accounting system will be developed later in response to the new manufacturing environment. This approach is more readily acceptable to a firm such as GRSW because it does not have the financial reporting paradigms of a publicly held organization. Regardless of the size of an organization or whether it's publicly or privately owned, these same few

financial measurements are adaptable to any financial environment.

A WORLD-CLASS CULTURE

There are a number of specific lessons and conclusions that can be drawn from GRSW's experience. First, GRSW's focused approach to identifying constraints (i.e., the four + one program) allowed the company to identify its major problems and implement appropriate solutions. The company was able not only to achieve some early production and quality control advances, but it convinced employees that management was open to their suggestions and would assume the risks associated with any change. By allowing workers to identify the root causes of problems and propose solutions, GRSW realized the benefit of greater employee motivation and commitment to the solutions.

Second, the company addressed the conversion process by implementing both production and cultural changes. At GRSW machines were rearranged, tooling was improved, setup and cycle times were reduced, and preventive maintenance and housekeeping were improved. The cultural changes needed to support the new manufacturing environment also were addressed. Through an extensive process of employee training and communication, GRSW created an atmosphere where workers believed their ideas would be valued, listened to, and implemented. They became convinced that management was open to change and that conventional wisdom could be challenged. In short, the firm's commitment to employee training and involvement helped to create a culture at GRSW that supported the physical and production changes.

The last lesson to be gleaned from the GRSW story is the role that trust played in the conversion process. The trust that developed between management and their employees formed the connecting link between the production and cultural changes that were necessary to create a WCM environment.

In the final analysis, what occurred was not the result of the manufacturing characteristics of world-class manufacturing. The remarkable changes at GRSW took place because management was able to build trust and confidence with employees. Management listened, communicated, called on people, and responded in unusual and unconventional ways to employee needs. Grand Rapids Spring & Wire Co. created a world-class culture that said we trust and believe in our employees. ∎

MEETING EVALUATION

In order to measure whether or not any meeting is worth repeating or sending more associates to, we have an evaluation form. The forms are reviewed and we decide whether or not to continue funding such programs. We try to encourage everyone to examine the status quo: just because something exists does not mean it is worth keeping. By subjecting meetings to regular scrutiny, we have saved countless hours and energy by halting nonproductive gatherings.

Magic, Inc.

Meeting Evaluation

Meeting: _____   **Date:** _____

1 = Poor   2 = Fair   3 = Average   4 = Above Average   5 = Excellent

1.	Organization of the meeting	1	2	3	4	5
2.	Meeting content	1	2	3	4	5
3.	Interaction among participants	1	2	3	4	5
4.	Comfort of the meeting location	1	2	3	4	5
5.	Overall value to you	1	2	3	4	5

		Long				Right/Time
6.	Length of meeting	1	2	3	4	5

How could this and future meetings be improved?

The Magic Workbook, Michigan State University Press, 1999

HERBIE PROCESS

We derived the Herbie Process from the character in *The Goal.* Herbie was the boy scout who slowed down the hike to camp. Every organization has something that holds it back the most from reaching its goal. You will not significantly strengthen your organization without focusing on the weakest link.

At Magic we have developed the following Herbie Process:

- Everyone spends one hour listening to an overview of the concept of constraint management and the importance of focusing on the weakest link. After this, we start the Herbie Process, basically brainstorming sessions. In groups of fifteen to twenty, a facilitator lists each group's ideas of the company's Herbie. After all ideas are listed, each group votes on the top two.
- Key management people sit down and review all the Herbies one by one. We had over three hundred ideas listed by approximately ninety people. It became apparent that we had a large difference of opinion between management and associates on a good number of issues.
- Eventually we focused on five issues—housekeeping, sample board, setup reduction time, preventive maintenance, and materials. Focus groups began to address these areas. Each focus group was given a mission statement and training on how to run meetings. A facilitator participated in the focus group meetings for a period of time to assure that the groups were functioning reasonably well.
- The president sat down with each group and reviewed its list of Herbies. The perception gaps were closed, and many rumors were killed on the spot. The president also discussed any other issue the group thought important. The groups were then informed of the issues we were going to focus on and how we were going to go about it. This part of the process helped to build additional trust and understanding. The associates' ideas were being addressed.
- Everyone in the company was asked over and over what our five main issues were and what we were doing about them. Significant improvements started to appear. The company's pride and associates' morale soared because the associates had the ideas and were making the changes.
- Approximately eighteen months later, we repeated the process. The groups identified fewer issues, but the issues mentioned were more significant. This time two additional items were added to our focus list—total quality management and culture. Two focus groups were established to address these two broad areas. The Herbie Process results have been excellent.

Last Things

We sincerely hope that both the story *It's Not Magic* and *The Magic Workbook* will help you improve your organization. We intend to update the *Workbook* as we learn more and as we hear from readers—and we truly hope that we will hear from you. The real Magic, Inc. has changed enormously, but change is a process that never ends. If we have learned anything, we have learned this. Improvement is not a one-time affair.

The process of change and transformation will never begin, however, until you decide that it should.

All the books and forms and charts and hints and ideas in the world will not overcome simple inertia or fear. You must begin the process yourself. We firmly believe that many organizations in the United States still need to begin to change. The story of Magic first establishing a culture began years ago when we decided that not to change meant not to survive. So we leave you with one final image. Begin to change now. In a few years you will not understand why you waited so long!

Magic, Inc

DO NOT WAIT
UNTIL YOU ARE
FORCED TO CHANGE!